LECTURE NOTEBOOK

LECTURE NOTEBOOK

Peter Smith

Lecturer in Economics
University of Southampton

McGRAW-HILL BOOK COMPANY

London • New York • St Louis • San Francisco • Auckland
Bogotá • Caracas • Lisbon • Madrid • Mexico
Milan • Montreal • New Delhi • Panama • Paris • San Juan
São Paulo • Singapore • Sydney • Tokyo • Toronto

Published by:

McGRAW-HILL Book Company Europe
Shoppenhangers Road, Maidenhead, Berkshire, SL6 2QL, England
Telephone 0628 23432
Fax 0628 770224

Copyright © 1994 McGraw-Hill International (UK) Limited. All rights reserved. No part of this publication may be reproduced, stored in a retrieval system, or transmitted, in any form or by any means, electronic, mechanical, photocopying, recording, or otherwise, without the prior permission of McGraw-Hill International (UK) Limited.

Printed and bound in Great Britain by
BPC Hazell Books Ltd
A member of
The British Printing Company Ltd

Note to the student

The *Lecture Notebook* is based upon the *Overhead Projection Transparencies* and is numbered accordingly.

The figure numbers which are italicized and set within parens within the slide captions refer to the main text BEGG, FISCHER and DORNBUSCH *Economics fourth edition.*

NOTES

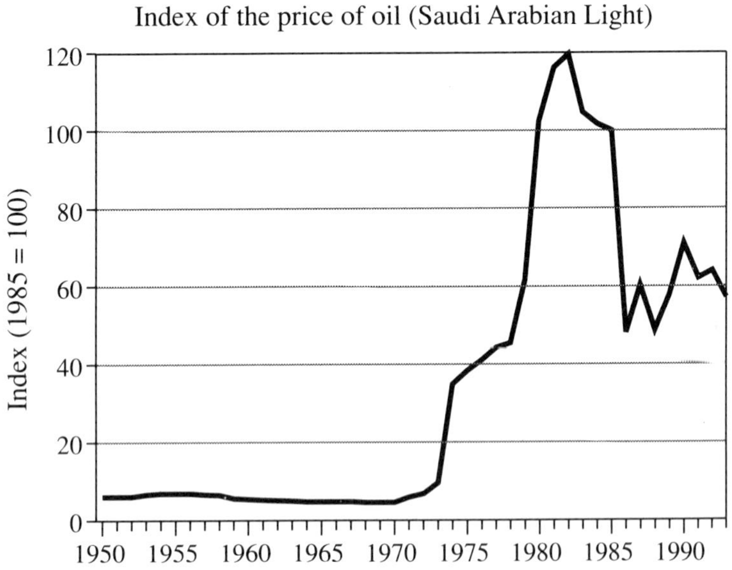

Index of the price of oil (Saudi Arabian Light)

Slide 1   What is economics?

Scarcity forces economic choices to be made.

Most countries are mixed economies, but the role of government differs widely between societies.

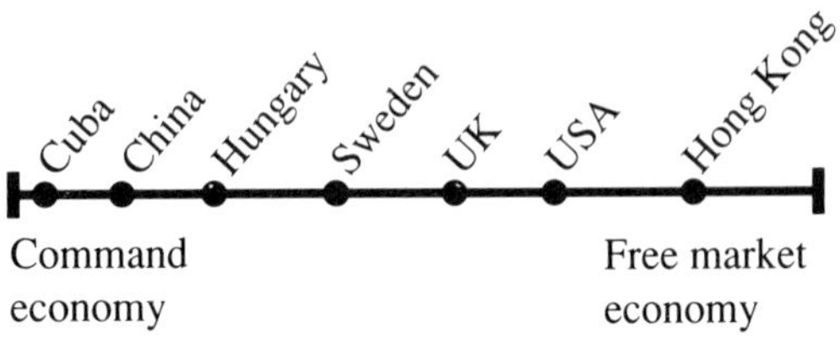

Slide 2   Scarcity and resource allocation *(Figure 1-4)*

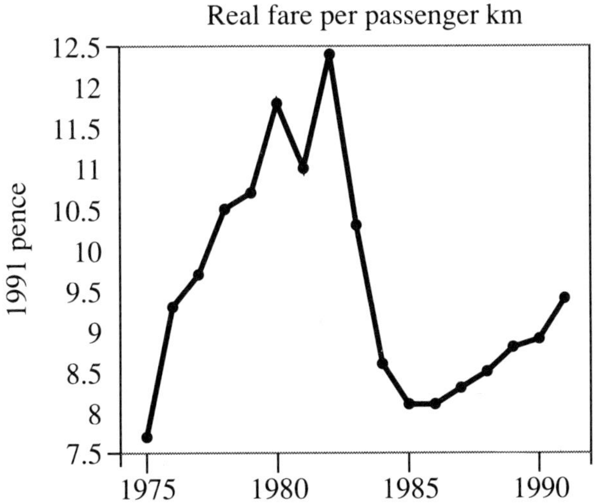

Real fare per passenger km

Slide 4   Models and data

NOTES

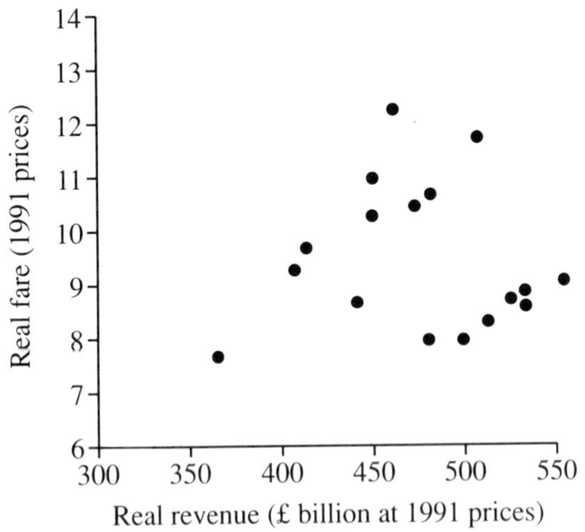

Real fare (1991 prices)

Real revenue (£ billion at 1991 prices)

Slide 5   Diagrams *(Figure 2-3)*

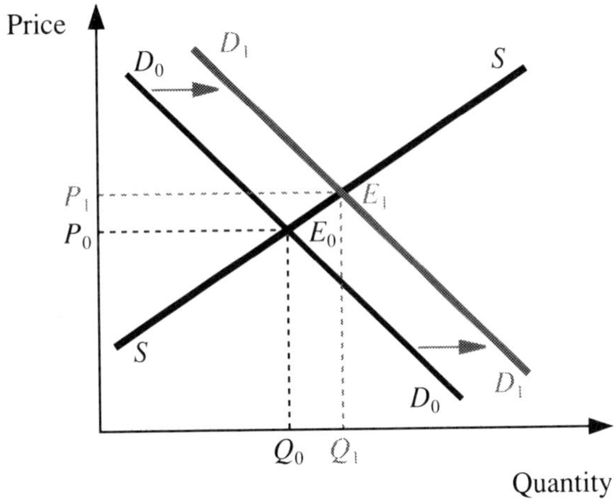

Price

D_0 D_1 S

P_1 E_1
P_0 E_0

S

D_0 D_1

Q_0 Q_1

Quantity

Slide 7   Market equilibrium — a demand shift

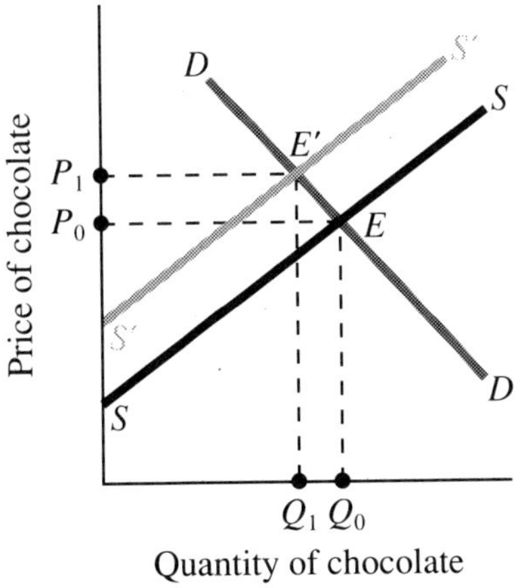

Price of chocolate

D S' S

P_1 E'
P_0 E

S'

D

S

Q_1 Q_0

Quantity of chocolate

Slide 8   A supply shift *(Figure 3-5)*

NOTES

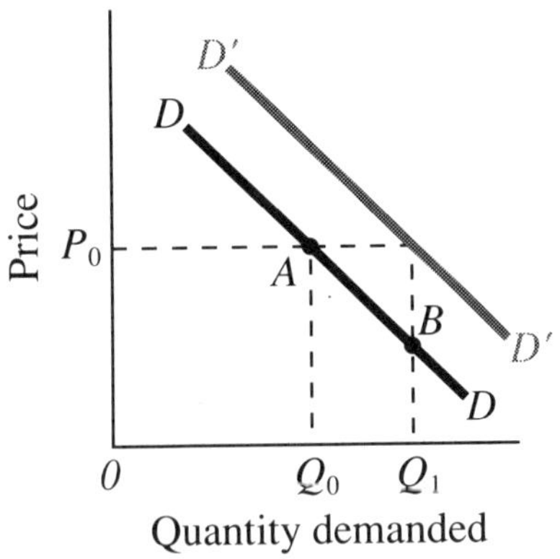

Slide 9 **An important distinction** *(Box 3-1)*

Governments sometimes impose PRICE CEILINGS, preventing producers from setting high prices needed to clear the market.

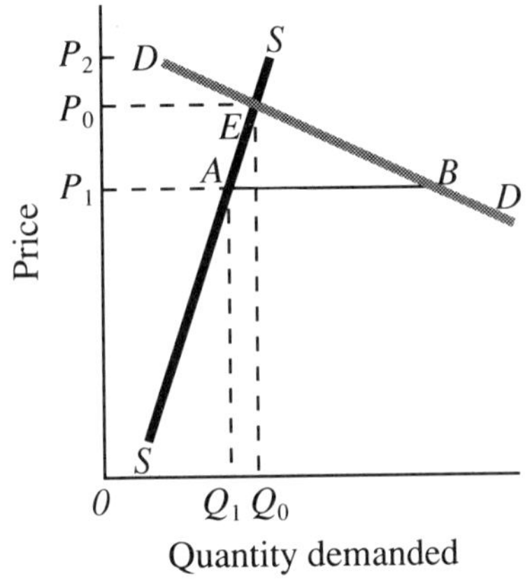

Slide 10 **A market in disequilibrium** *(Figure 3-7)*

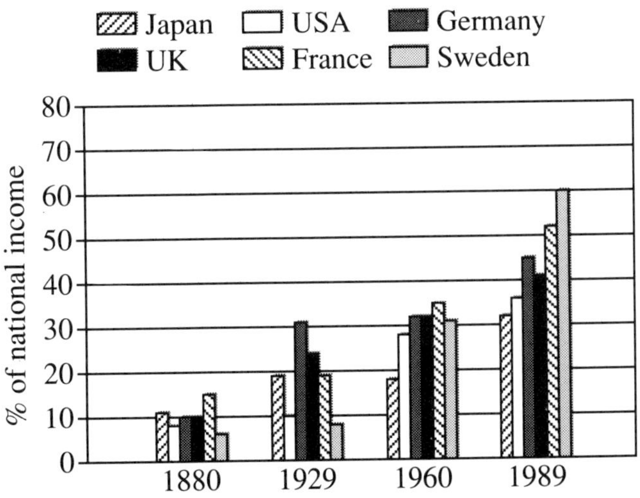

Slide 11 **What do governments do?** *(Table 4-2)*

NOTES

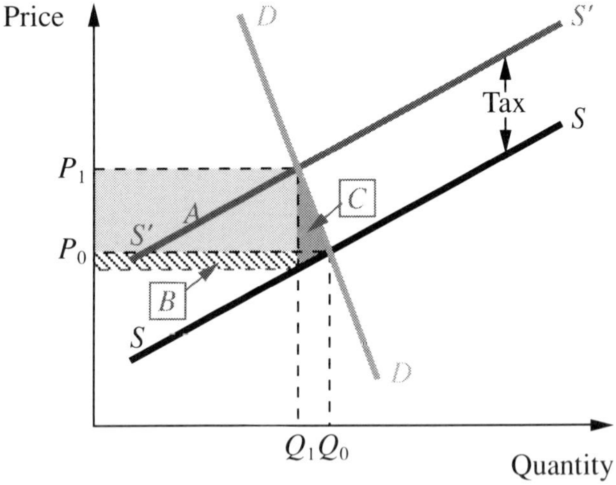

Slide 13   Who pays a commodity tax? *(Box 4-1)*

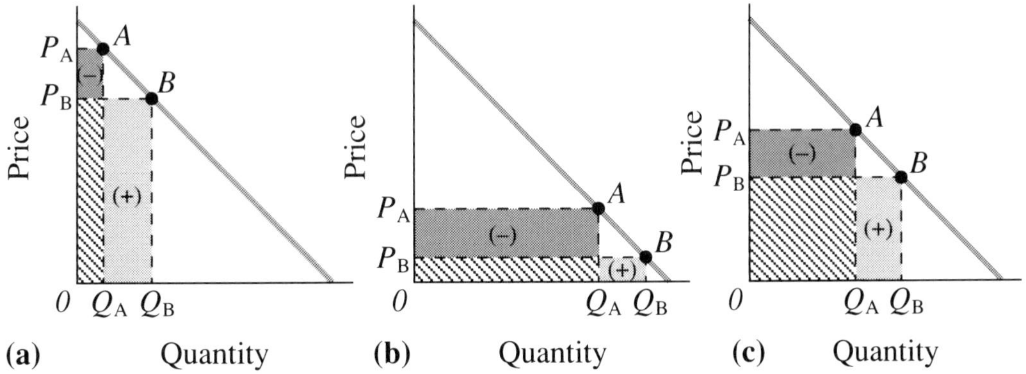

Slide 16   Price, quantity demanded and total expenditure *(Figure 5-4)*

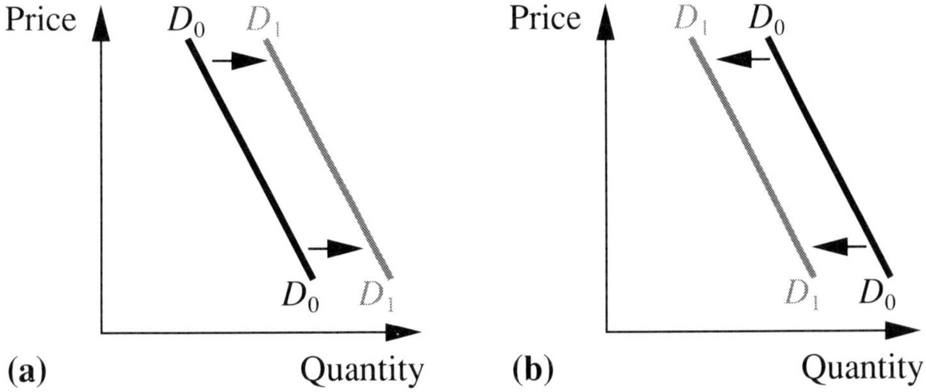

(a)   Quantity   **(b)**   Quantity   **(c)**   Quantity

(a)   Quantity   **(b)**   Quantity

Slide 19   The effect of income on demand

7

NOTES

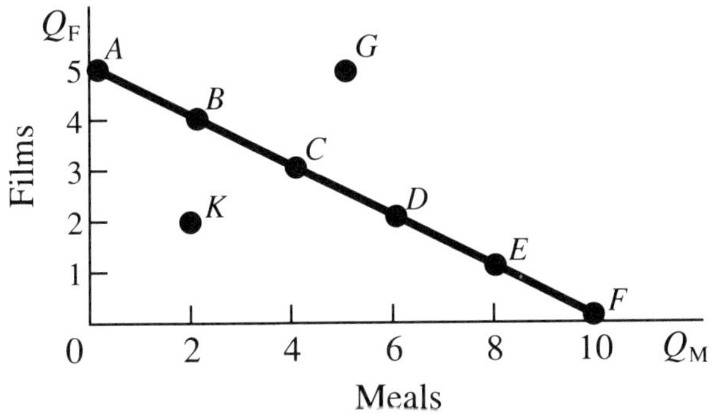

Slide 20   Elements of consumer choice theory *(Figure 6-1)*

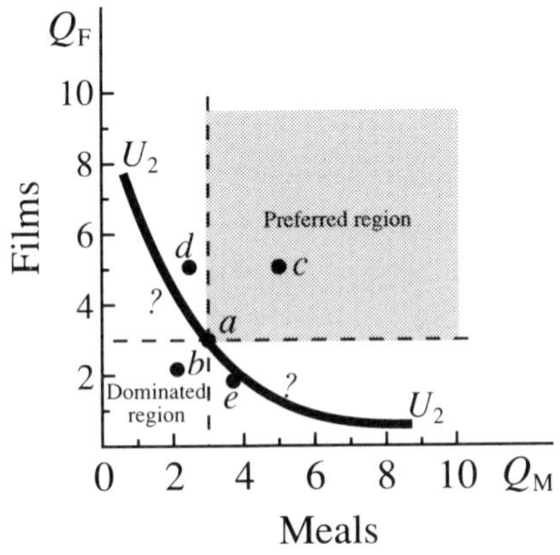

Slide 21   Consumer preferences *(Figure 6-2)*

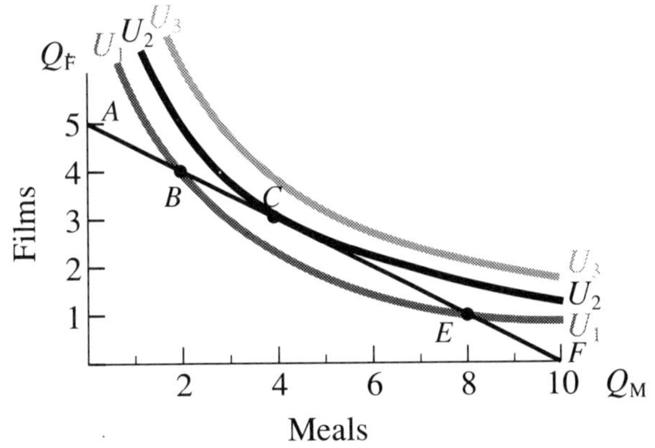

Slide 22   The consumer's choice *(Figure 6-6)*

NOTES

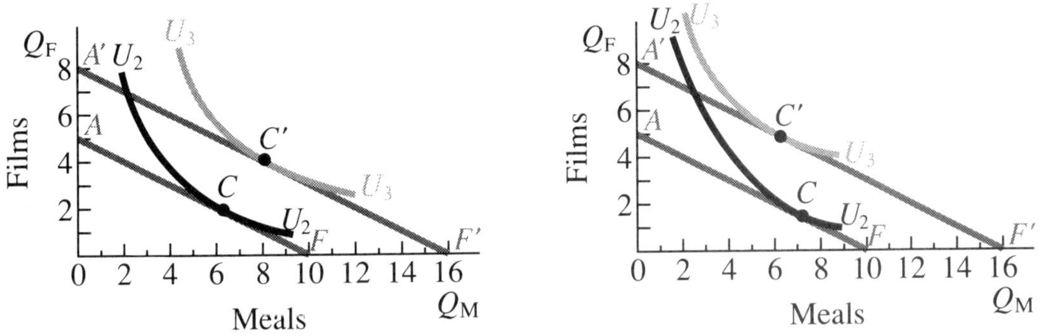

Slide 23   **Adjustment to income changes** *(Figures 6-8 & 6-9)*

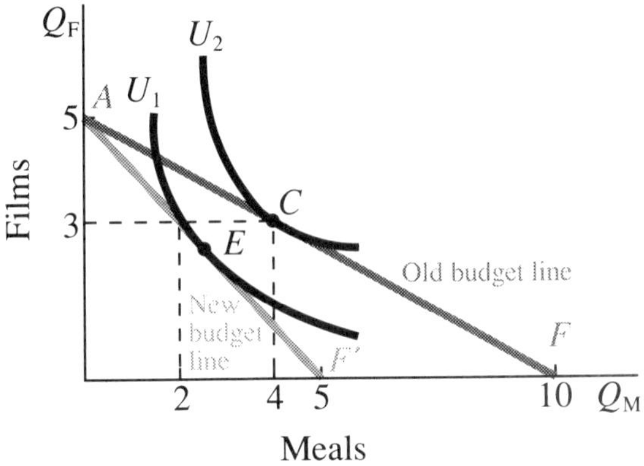

Slide 24   **Adjustment to price changes** *(Figure 6-10)*

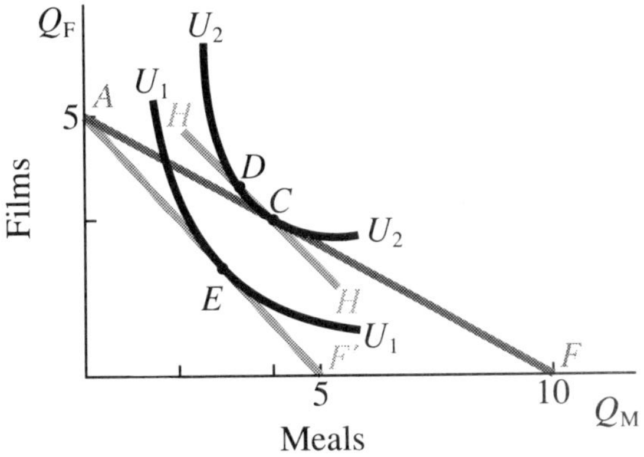

Slide 25   **Adjustment to price changes — the effects** *(Figure 6-11)*

NOTES

Snark International Balance Sheet			
31 December 1993			
ASSETS		LIABILITIES	
Cash	£40 000	Accounts payable	£90 000
Accounts receivable	70 000	Salaries payable	50 000
Inventories	100 000	Mortgage from insurance company	150 000
Factory building (original value £250 000)	200 000	Bank loan	60 000
			350 000
Other equipment (original value £300 000)	180 000		
		Net worth	240 000
	590 000		590 000

Slide 27   The firm's balance sheet *(Figure 7-3)*

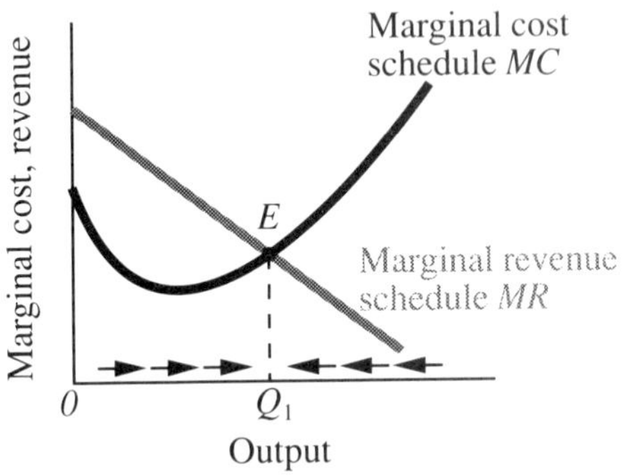

Slide 28   The firm's production decision *(Figure 7-8)*

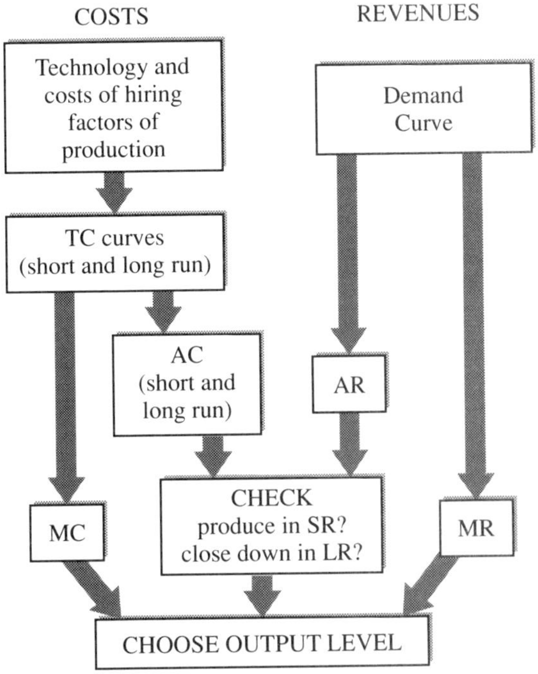

Slide 29   Choosing output

13

NOTES

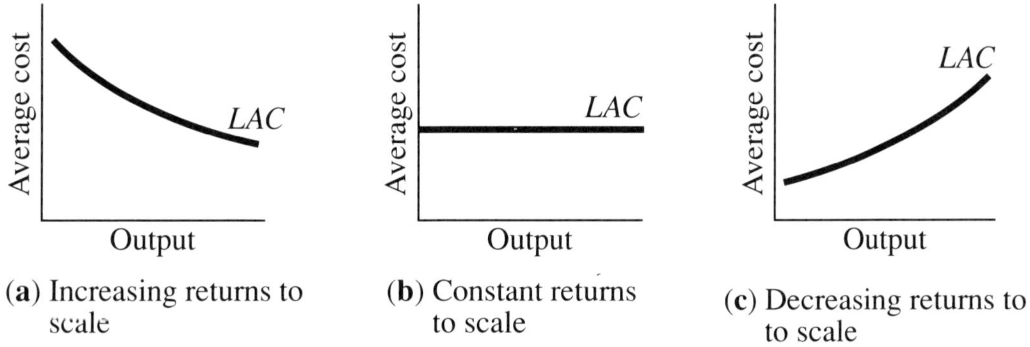

(a) Increasing returns to scale (b) Constant returns to scale (c) Decreasing returns to scale

Slide 31 Returns to scale and the long-run AC curve *(Figure 8-3)*

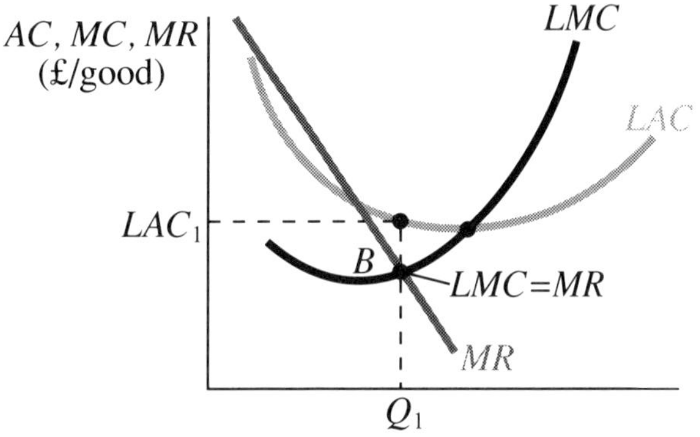

Slide 31 Returns to scale and the long-run AC curve *(Figure 8-6)*

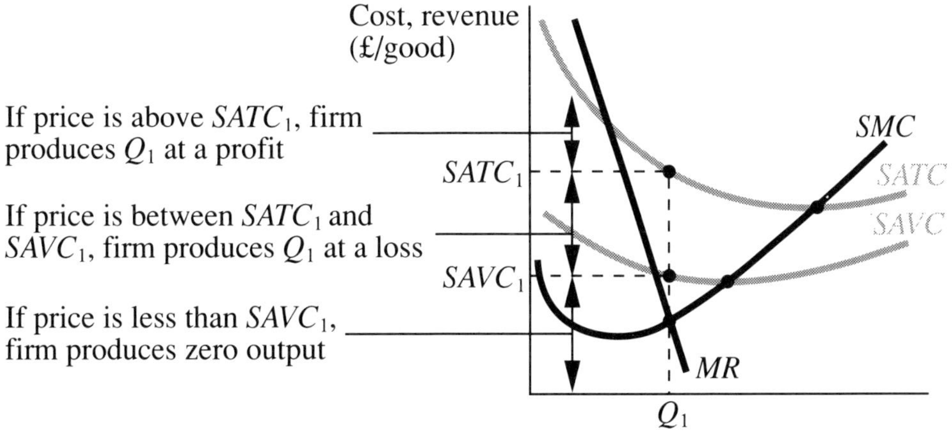

If price is above $SATC_1$, firm produces Q_1 at a profit

If price is between $SATC_1$ and $SAVC_1$, firm produces Q_1 at a loss

If price is less than $SAVC_1$, firm produces zero output

Slide 33 The firm's short-run output decision (2) *(Figure 8-9, Table 8-10)*

NOTES

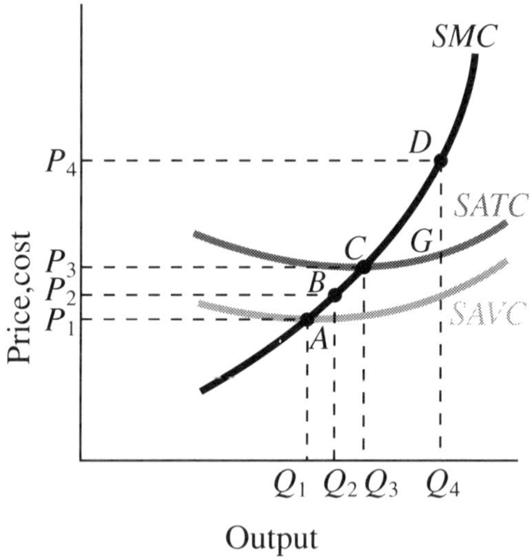

Slide 34   Perfect competition (1) *(Figure 9-2)*

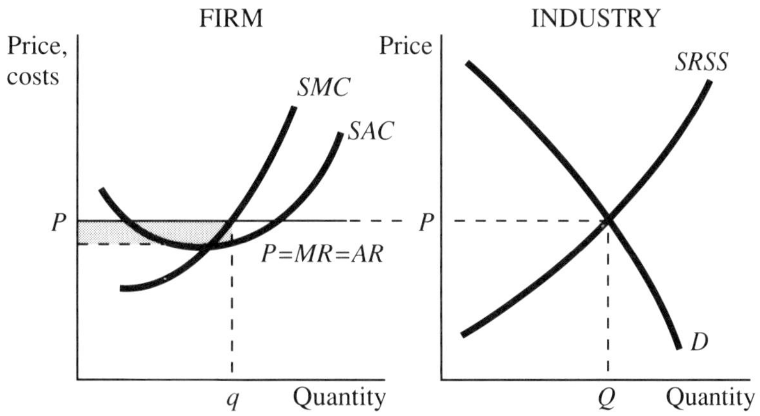

Slide 35   Perfect competition (2)

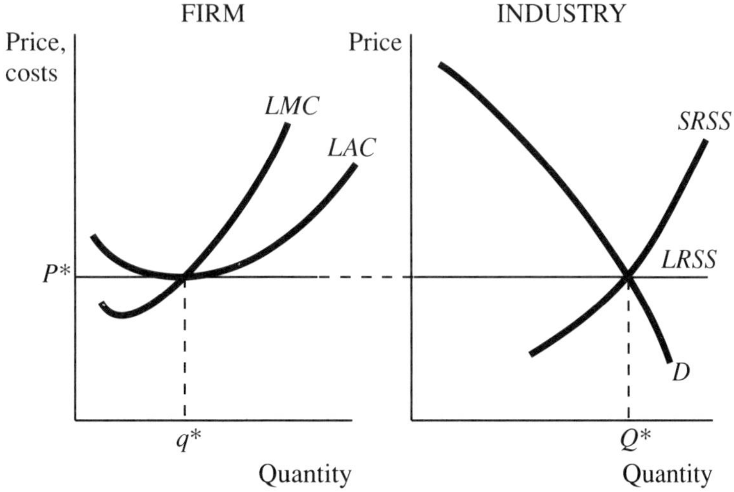

Slide 36   Perfect competition (3)

17

NOTES

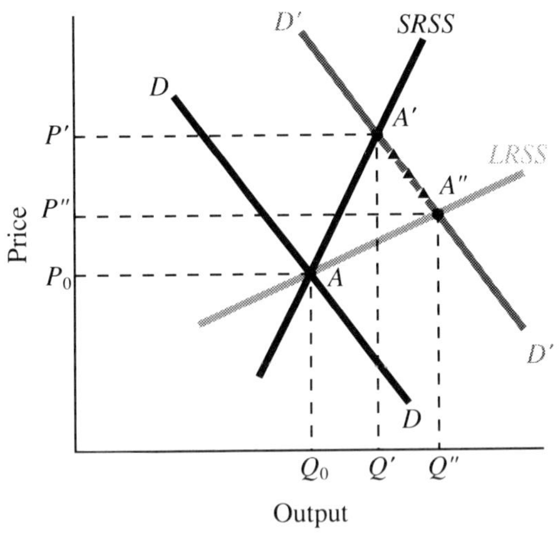

Slide 37   **The reaction of a competitive industry to an increase in market demand** *(Figure 9-10)*

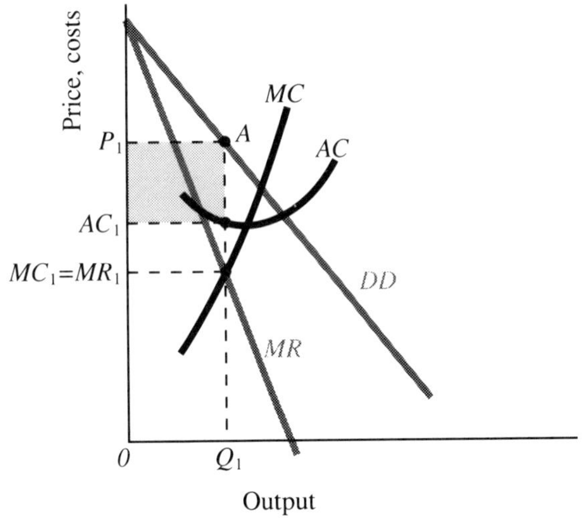

Slide 38   **Monopoly** *(Figure 9-13)*

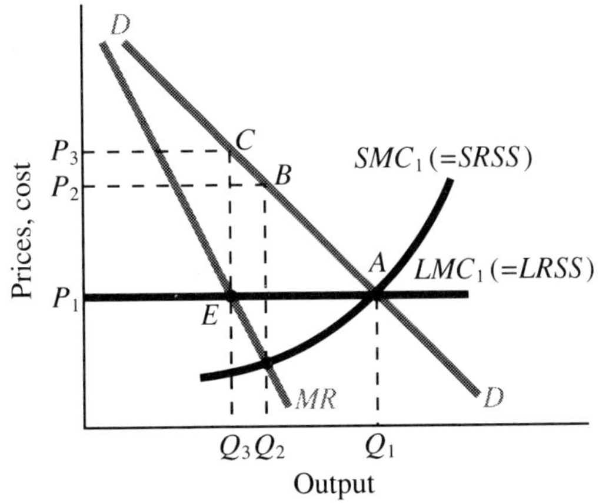

Slide 39   **Comparing monopoly with perfect competition** *(Figure 9-14)*

19

NOTES

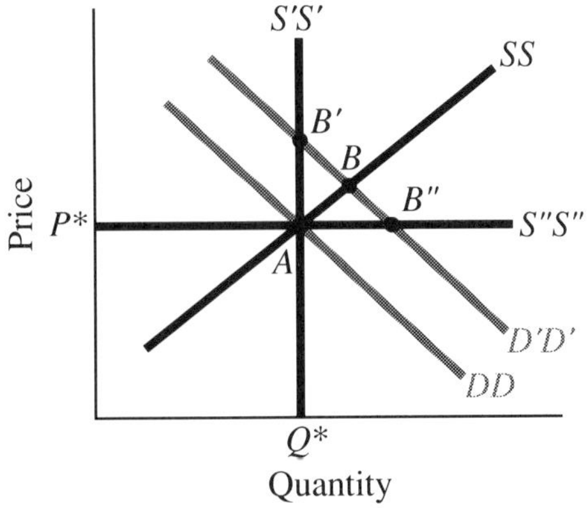

Slide 40   The elasticity of supply *(Box 9-1)*

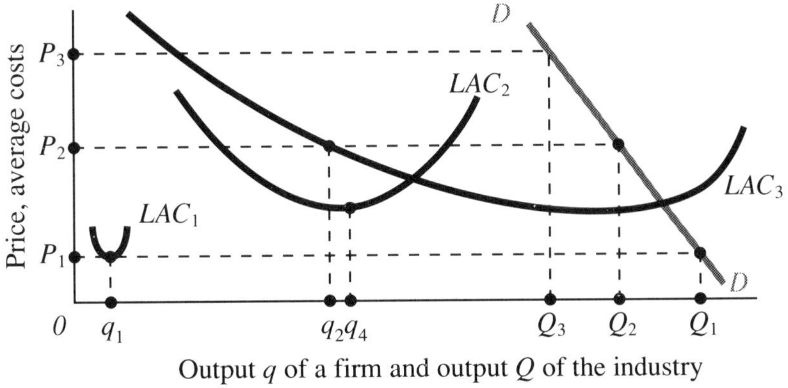

Slide 41   Forms of market structure *(Table 10-1, Figure 10-1)*

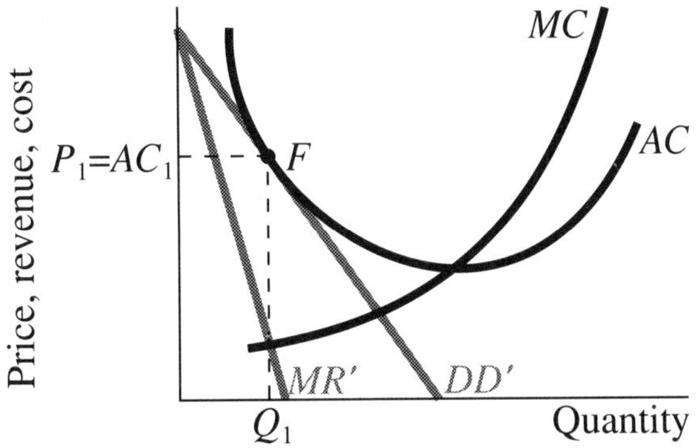

Slide 42   Monopolistic competition *(Figure 10-2)*

21

NOTES

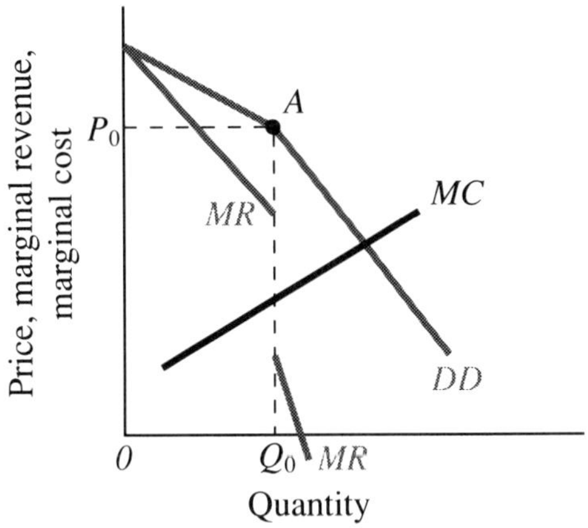

Slide 43   Oligopoly (1) *(Figure 10-4)*

		Firm B output			
		High		**Low**	
Firm A output	High	1	**1**	3	**0**
	Low	0	**3**	2	**2**

Slide 44   Oligopoly (2) *(Figure 10-5)*

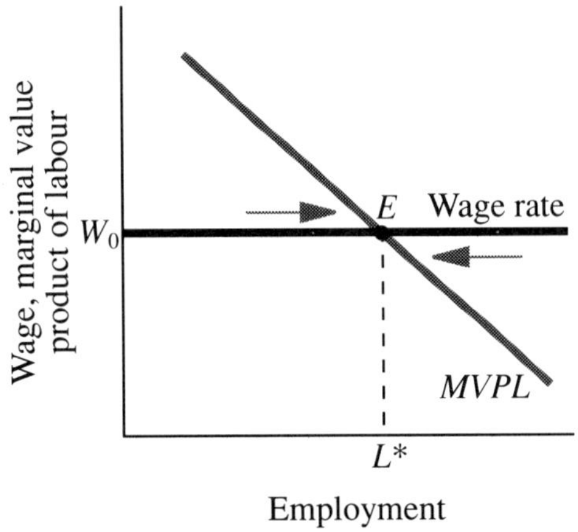

Slide 45   The demand for labour *(Figure 11-2)*

23

NOTES

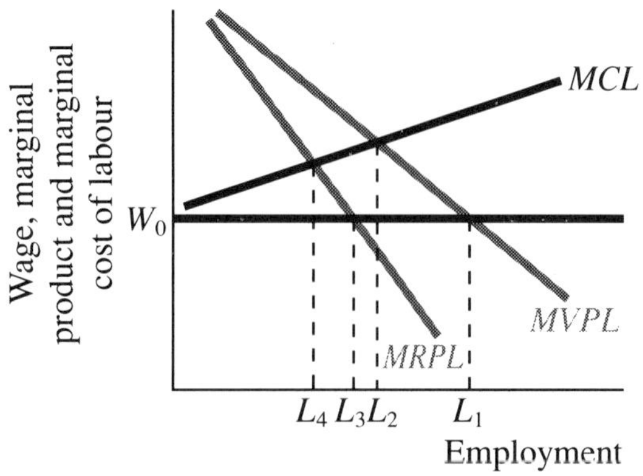

Slide 46 Monopoly and monopsony power *(Figure 11-3)*

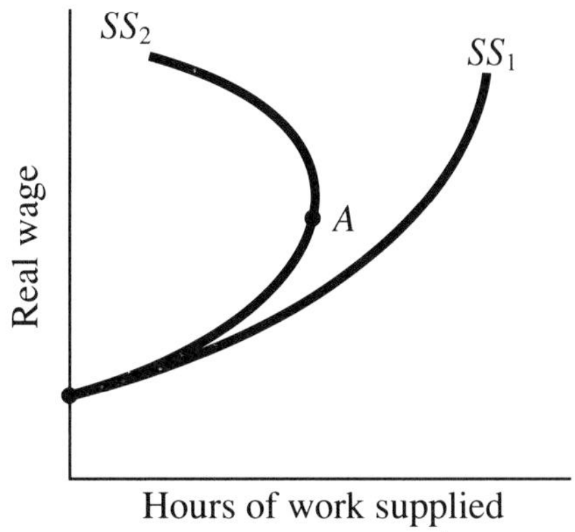

Wage, marginal product and marginal cost of labour

MCL

W_0

$MVPL$

$MRPL$

L_4 L_3 L_2 L_1

Employment

Slide 47 The supply of labour *(Figure 11-5)*

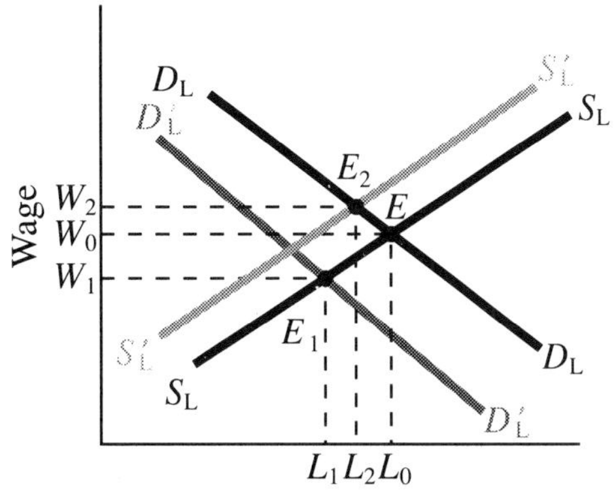

Real wage

SS_2

SS_1

A

Hours of work supplied

Slide 48 Industry labour market equilibrium *(Figure 11-7)*

Wage

D_L

D'_L

S'_L

S_L

E_2

E

W_2

W_0

W_1

S'_L

E_1

D_L

S_L

D'_L

$L_1 L_2 L_0$

Quantity of labour

25

NOTES

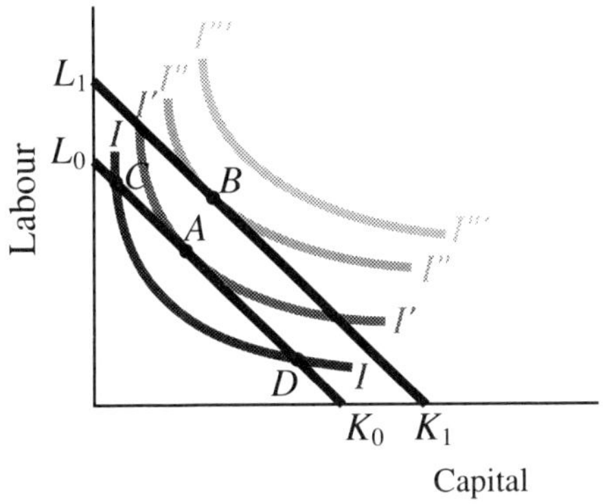

Slide 49   Cost minimization *(Figure 11-A2)*

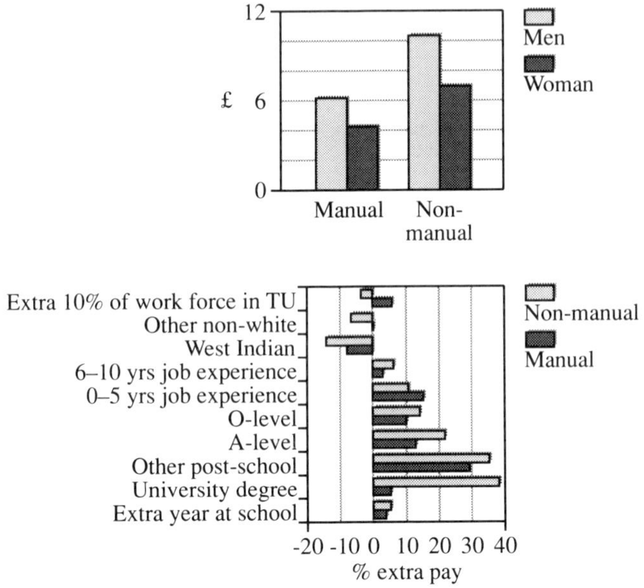

Slide 50   Pay differentials for men *(Tables 12-1 & 12-2)*

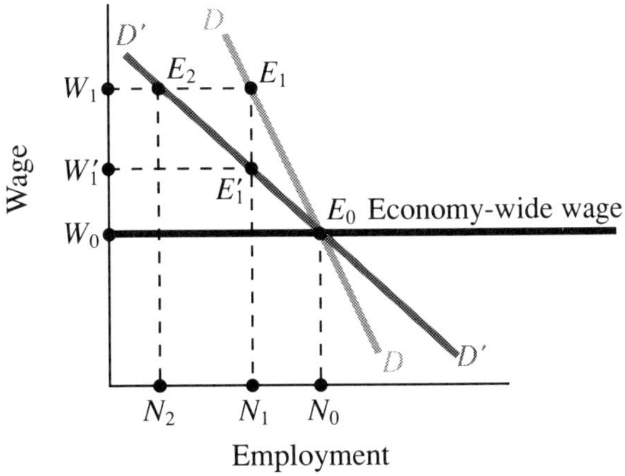

Slide 51   Trade unions *(Figure 12-6)*

27

NOTES

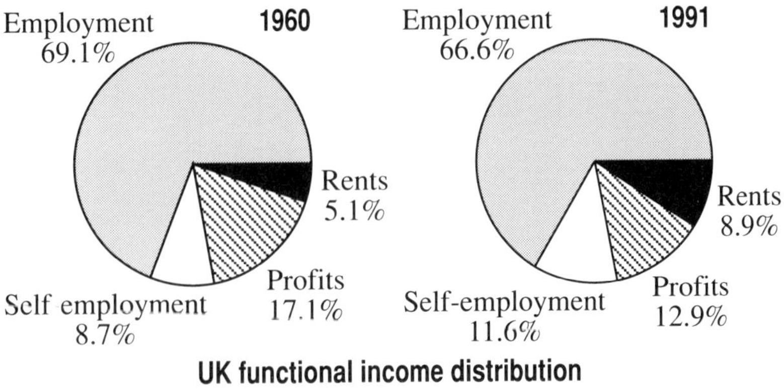

1960
Employment
69.1%
Rents
5.1%
Self employment
8.7%
Profits
17.1%

1991
Employment
66.6%
Rents
8.9%
Self-employment
11.6%
Profits
12.9%

UK functional income distribution

Slide 52   Capital

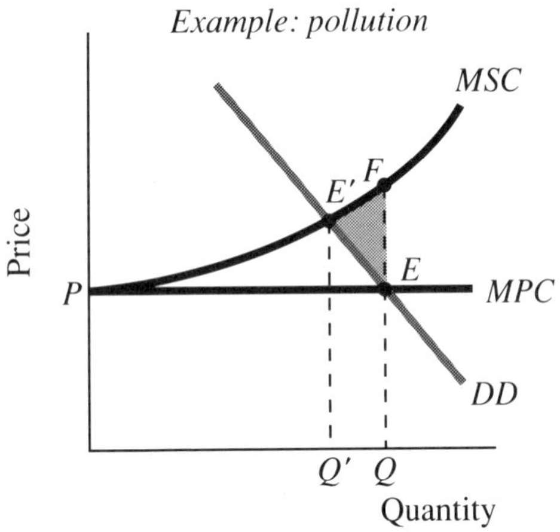

Example: pollution

MSC

E' F

P   E   MPC

DD

Q' Q
Quantity

Price

Slide 54   Externalities in production *(Figure 15-6)*

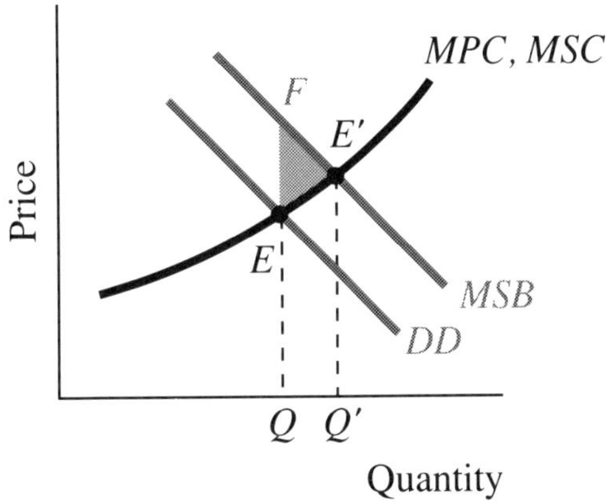

MPC, MSC

F   E'

E

MSB

DD

Q Q'

Quantity

Price

Slide 55   Externalities in consumption *(Figure 15-7)*

NOTES

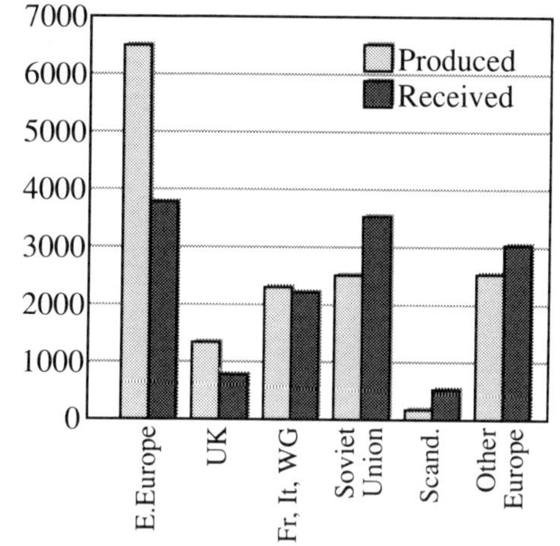

Slide 56 **Acid rain: a bitter controversy** *(Box 15-1)*

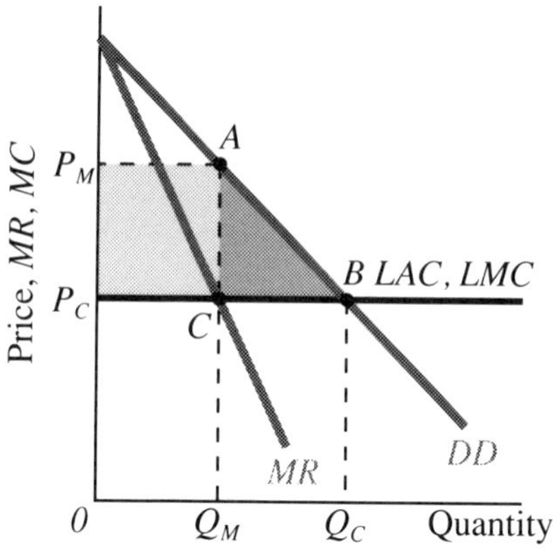

Slide 58 **The social cost of monopoly** *(Figure 17-1)*

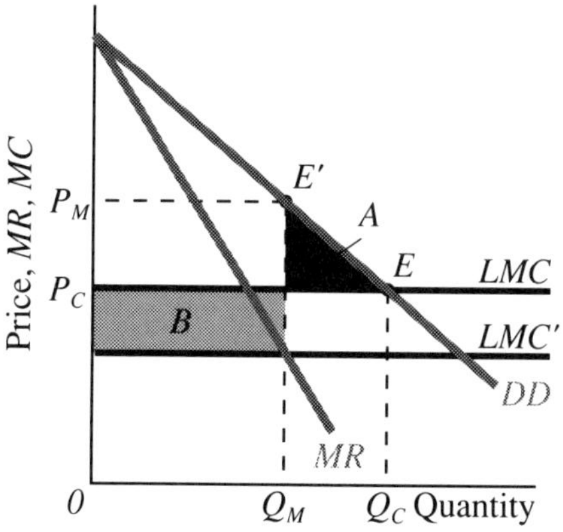

Slide 58 **The social cost of monopoly** *(Figure 17-2)*

NOTES

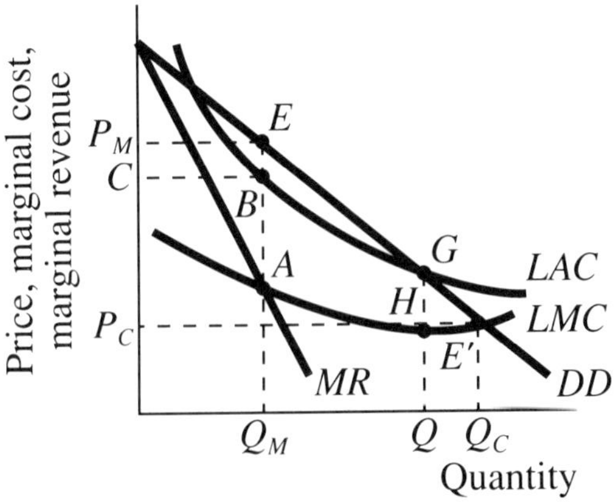

Slide 60   Natural monopoly *(Figure 17-4)*

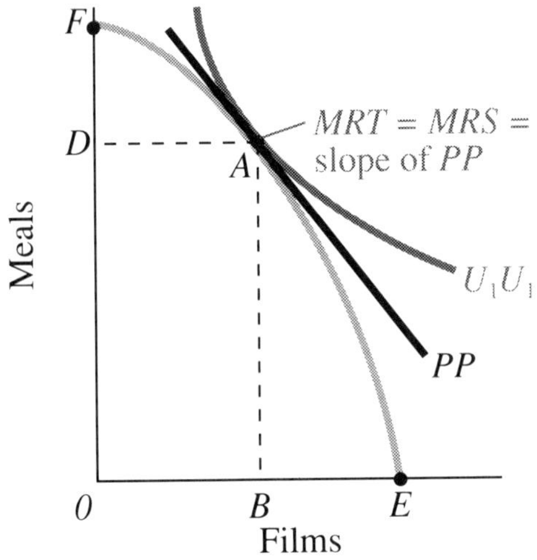

Slide 63   Productive and allocative efficiency *(Figure 19-4)*

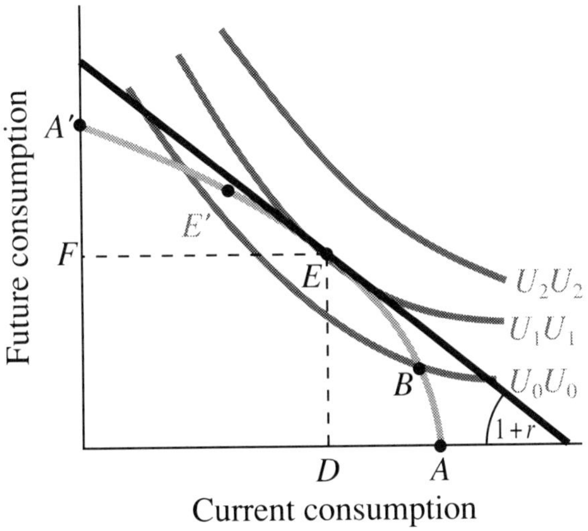

Slide 65   Saving, investment and the interest rate *(Figure 19-8)*

33

NOTES

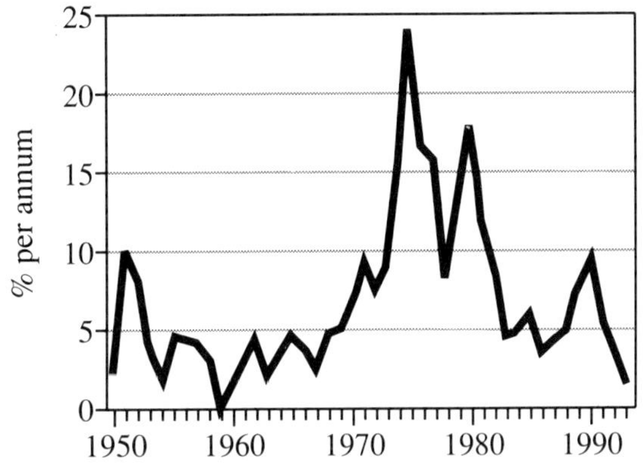

Slide 67   Inflation in the UK, 1950–90. *Source: CSO, Economic Trends, Employment Gazette*

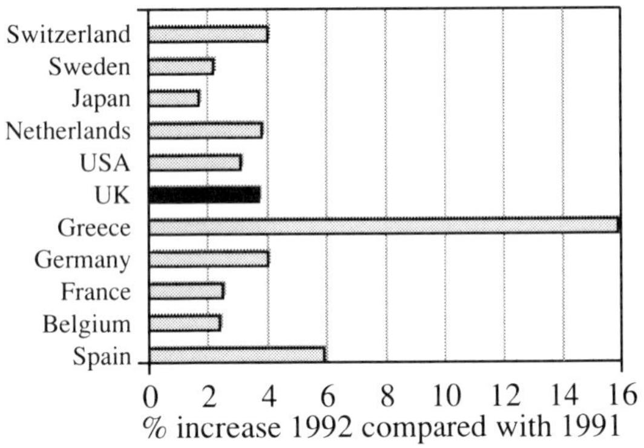

Slide 67   Inflation in selected OECD countries

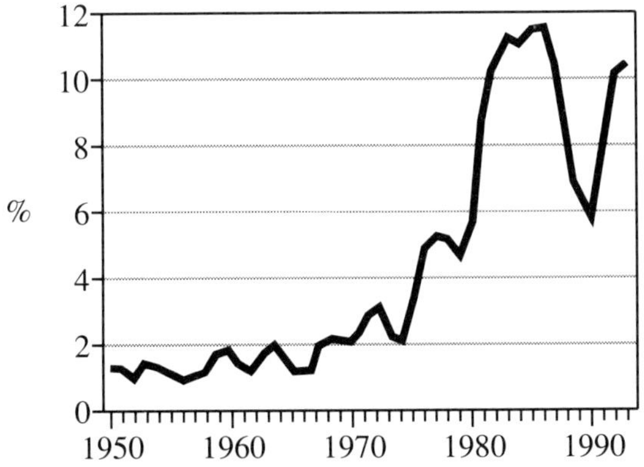

Slide 68   Unemployment in the UK, 1950–93

35

NOTES

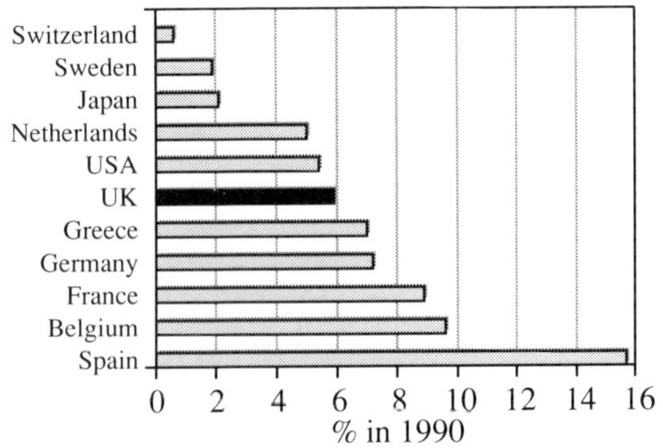

Slide 68   Unemployment in selected OECD countries

INFLATION   UNEMPLOYMENT   REAL GNP GROWTH

■ UK   □ USA   ▨ W Germany   ▨ Japan

Slide 69   Inflation, unemployment and real GNP growth *(Table 20-4)*

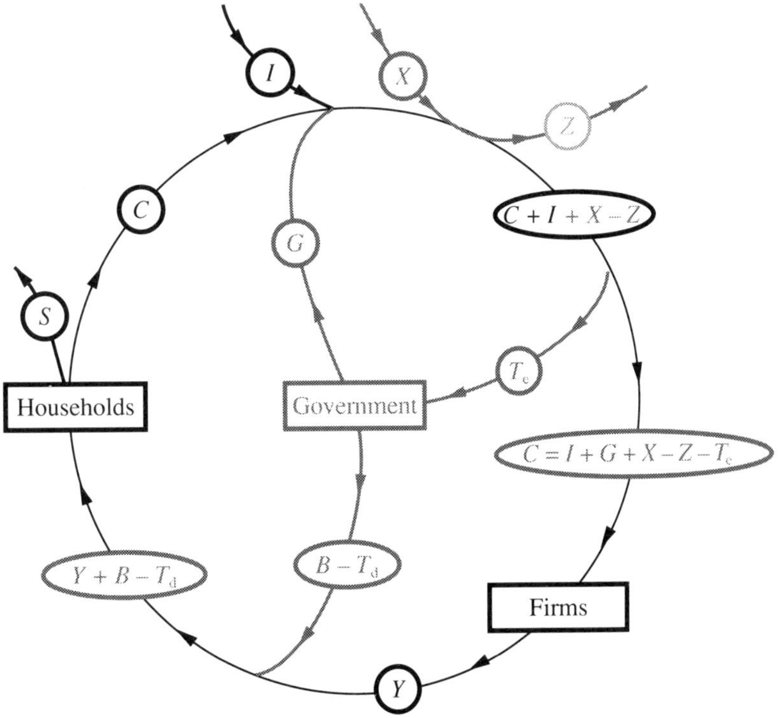

Slide 70   The circular flow *(Figure 20-4)*

37

NOTES

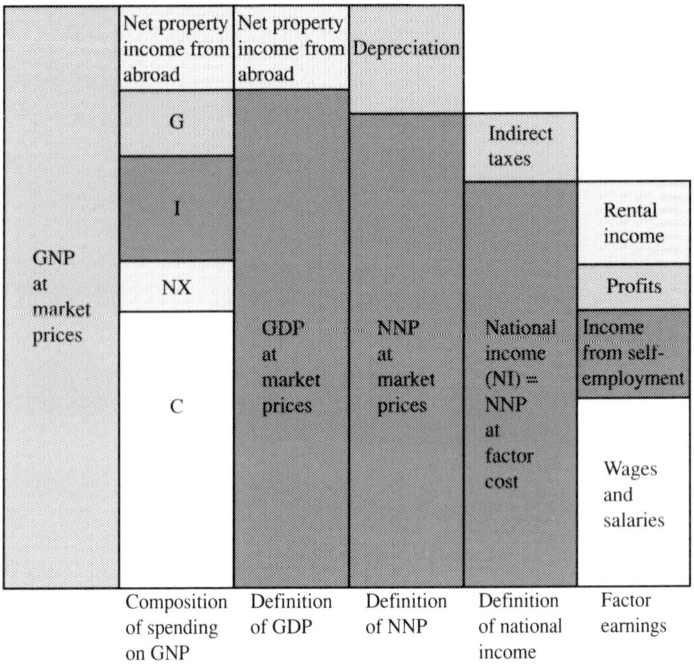

Slide 72 **National income — a summary** *(Figure 20-5)*

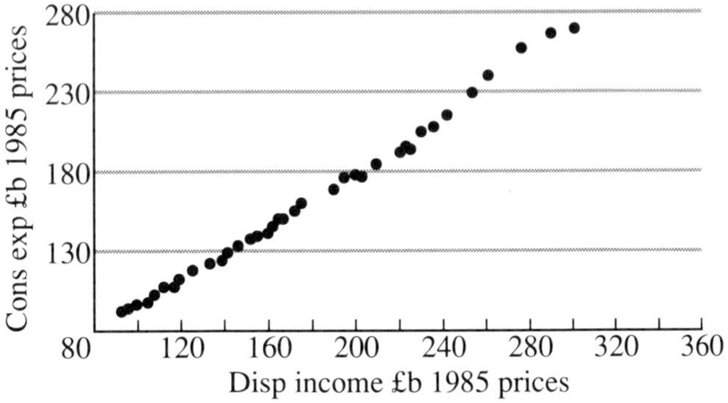

Slide 73 **Consumption demand**

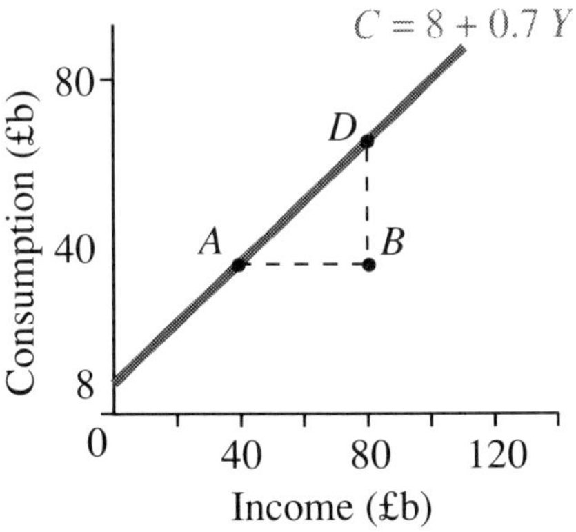

$$C = 8 + 0.7\,Y$$

Slide 74 **The consumption function** *(Figure 21-2)*

39

NOTES

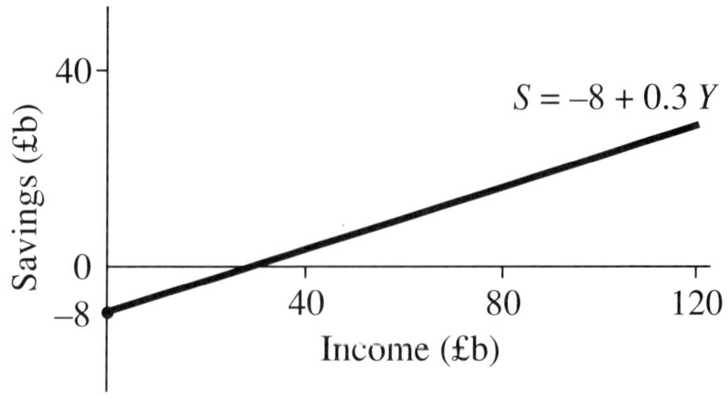

Slide 75   Savings *(Figure 21-3)*

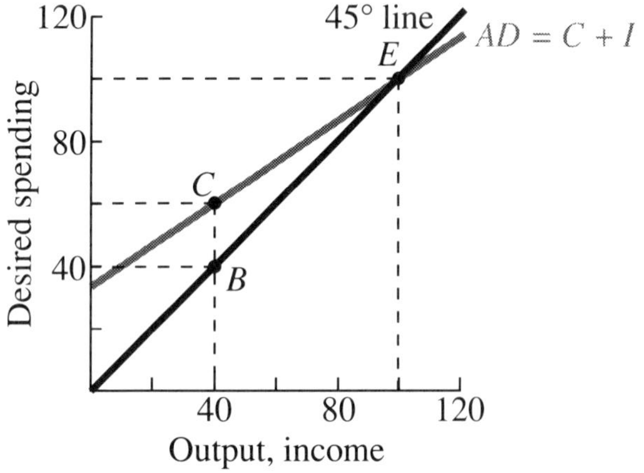

$S = -8 + 0.3\,Y$

Slide 76   Short-run equilibrium *(Figure 21-5)*

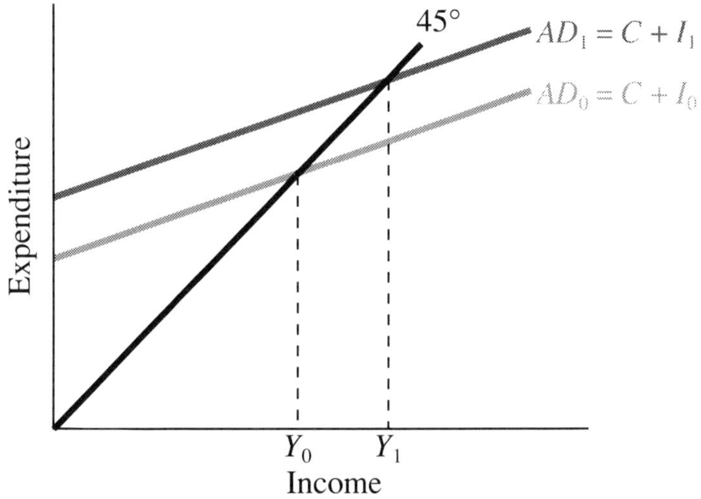

Slide 77   An increase in aggregate demand: the multiplier

41

NOTES

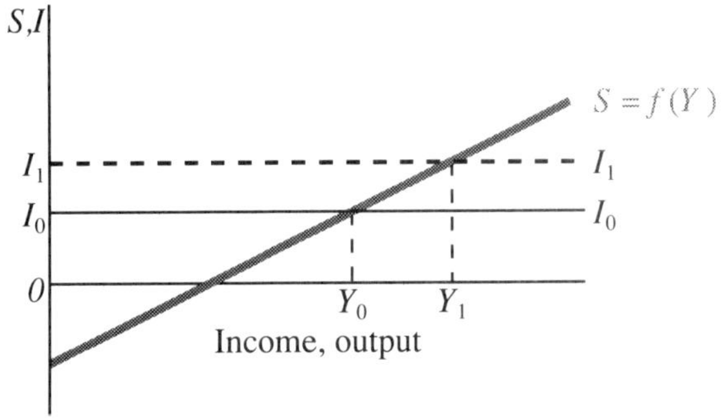

Slide 78 An alternative approach: savings and investment

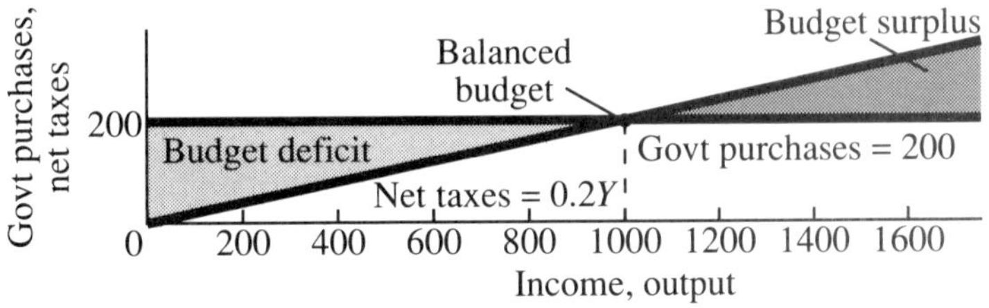

Slide 79 Government in the income expenditure model *(Figure 22-5)*

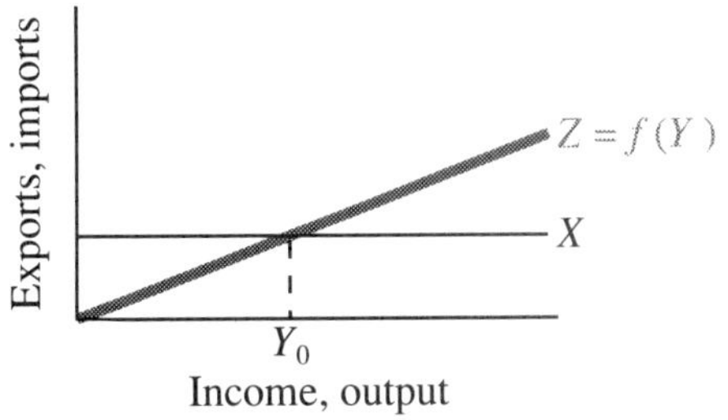

Slide 81 Foreign trade and income determination

NOTES

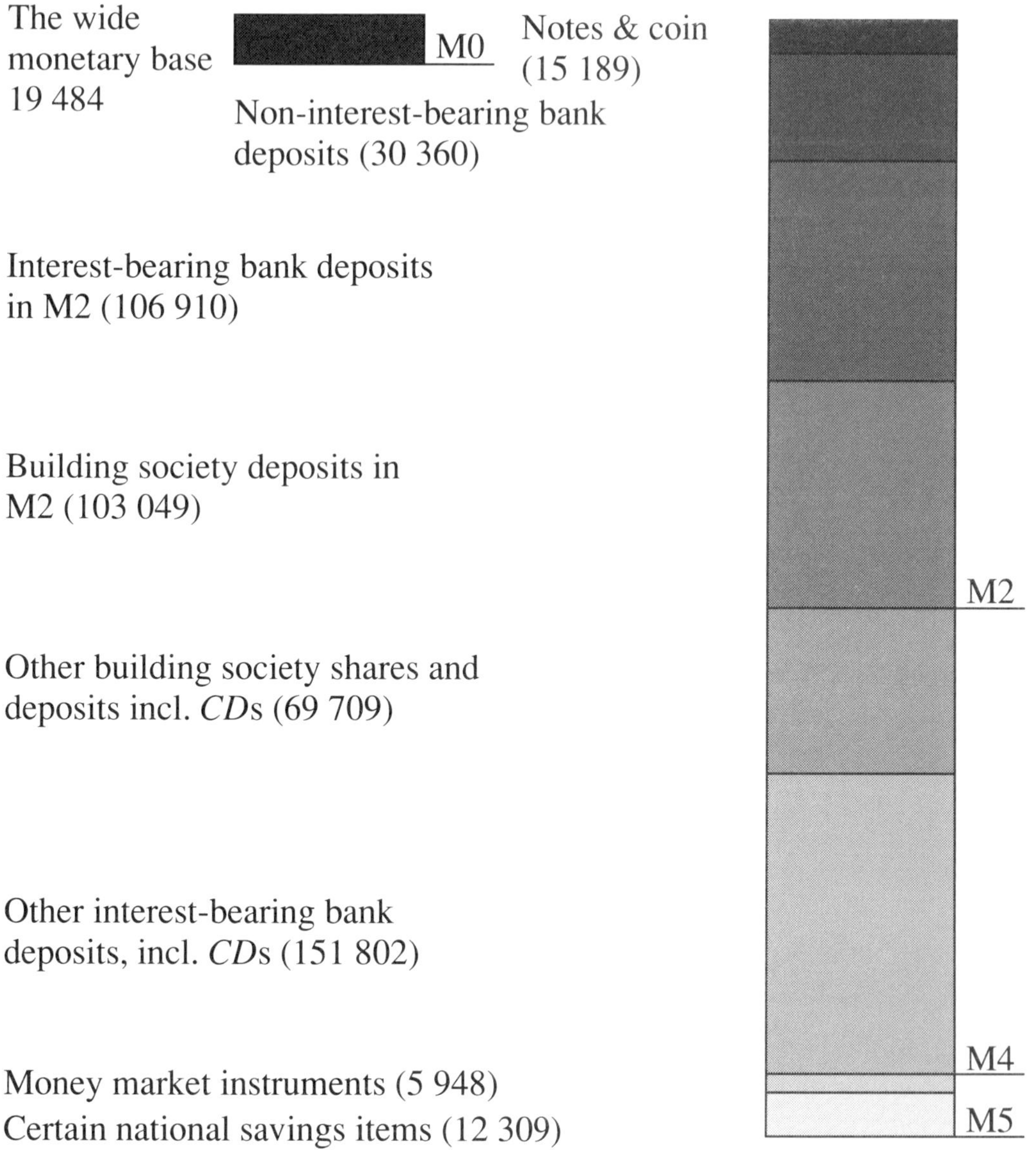

The wide
monetary base
19 484

M0   Notes & coin
(15 189)

Non-interest-bearing bank
deposits (30 360)

Interest-bearing bank deposits
in M2 (106 910)

Building society deposits in
M2 (103 049)

M2

Other building society shares and
deposits incl. *CD*s (69 709)

Other interest-bearing bank
deposits, incl. *CD*s (151 802)

M4

Money market instruments (5 948)

Certain national savings items (12 309)

M5

Slide 86   Definitions of money in the UK

NOTES

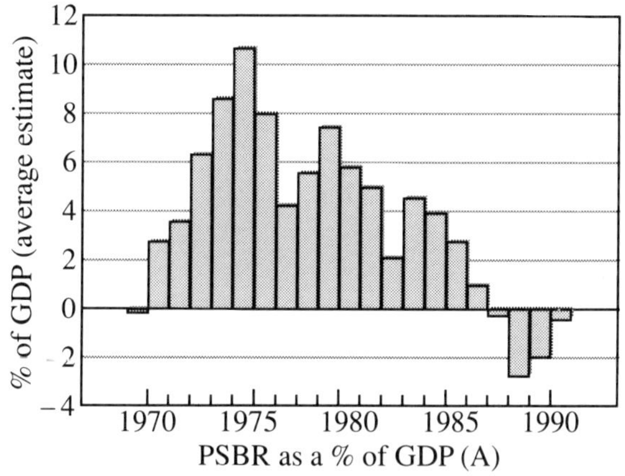

Slide 88 Other functions of the Central Bank *(Source: Economic Review Data Supplement 1991)*

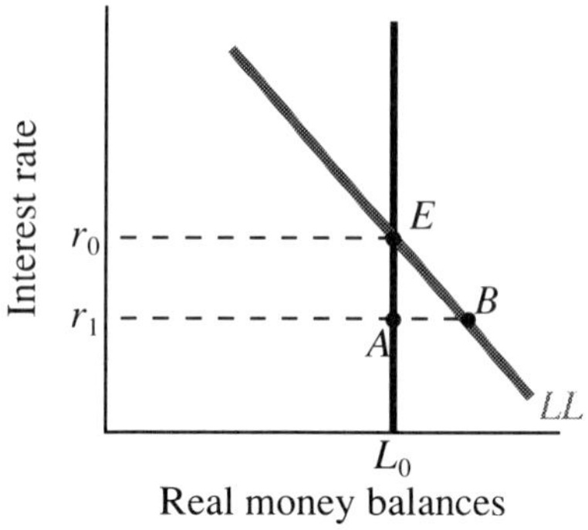

Slide 90 Money market equilibrium *(Figure 24-2)*

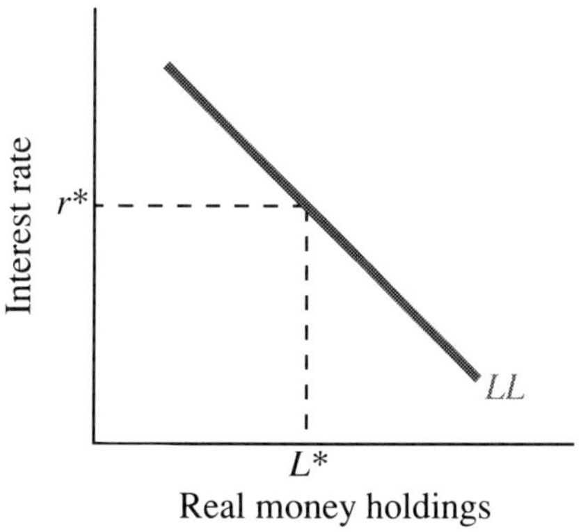

Slide 91 Monetary control

NOTES

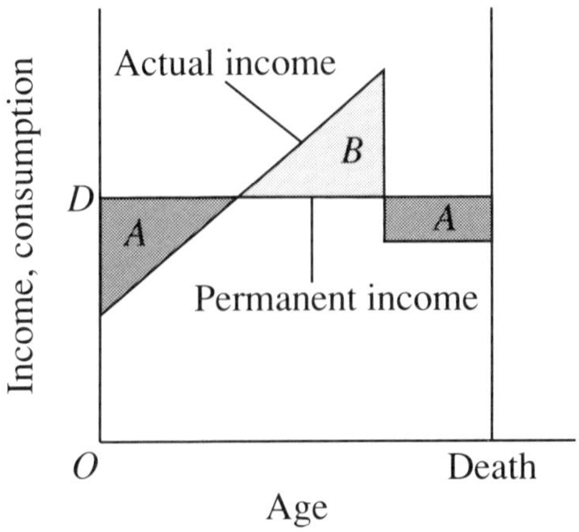

Slide 94 Consumption revisited *(Figure 25-1)*

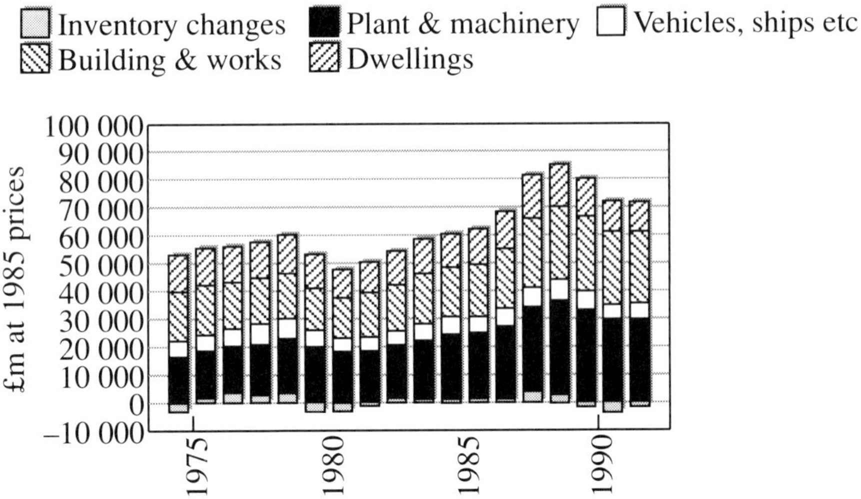

Slide 95 Investment *(Source: EJAS, MDS)*

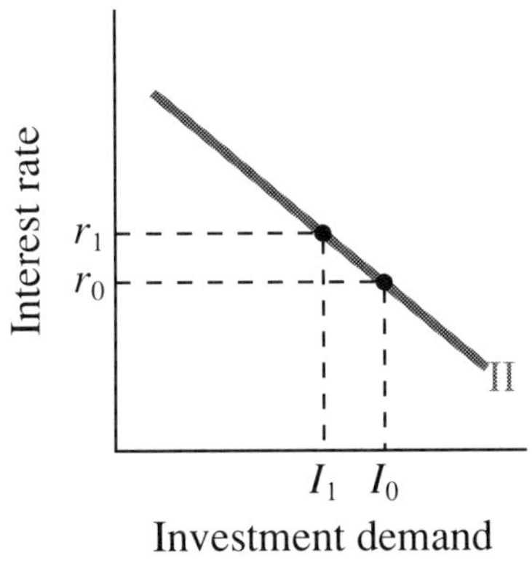

Slide 96 The demand for fixed investment *(Figure 25-3)*

49

NOTES

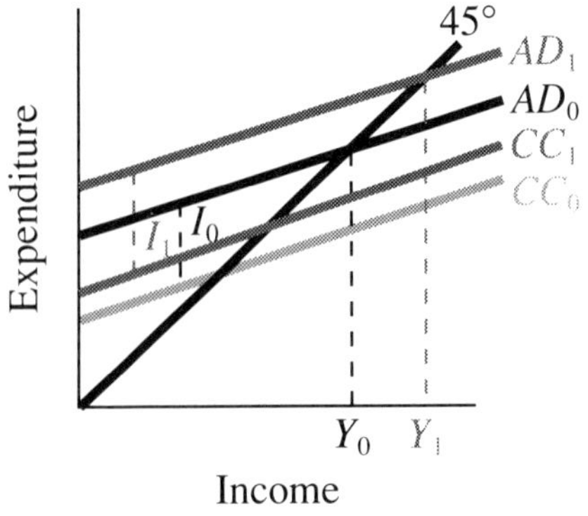

Slide 97   **Effects of an increase in the money supply**

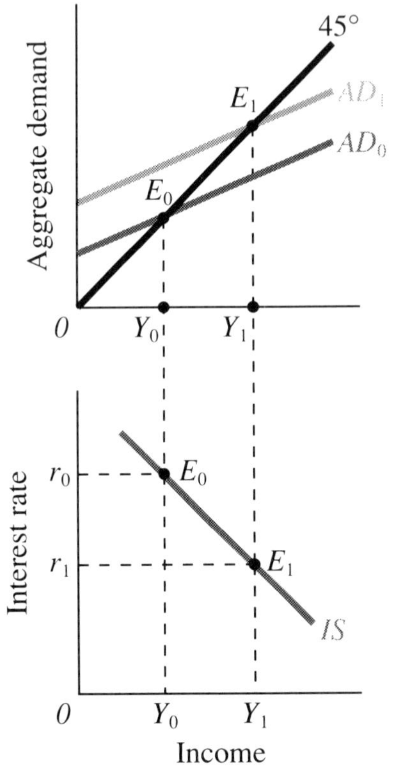

Slide 98   **The *IS* schedule: goods market equilibrium** *(Figure 25-6)*

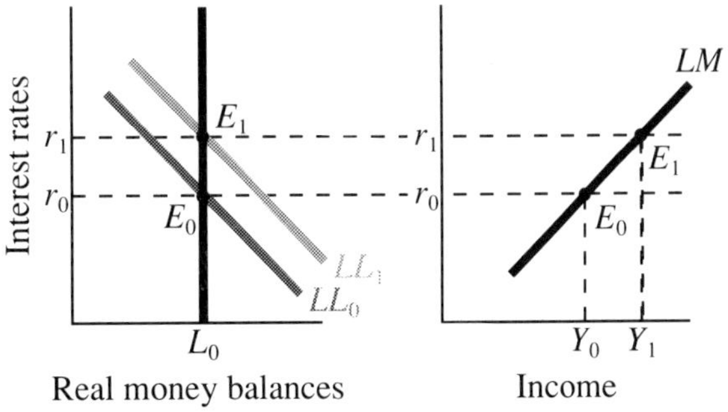

Slide 99   **The *LM* schedule: money market equilibrium** *(Figure 25-7)*

51

NOTES

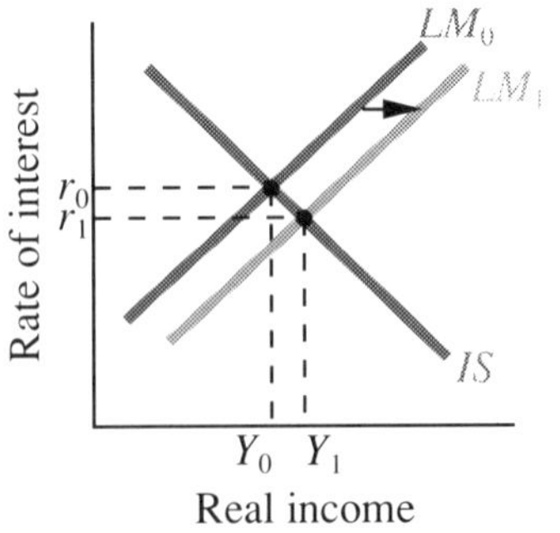

Slide 100 *IS-LM* and monetary policy

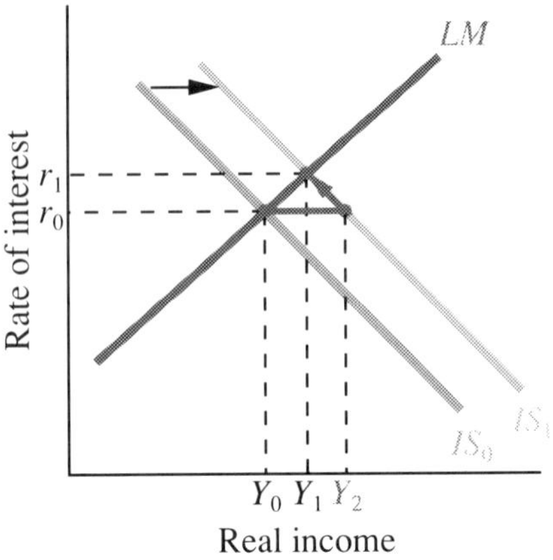

Slide 101 *IS-LM* and fiscal policy

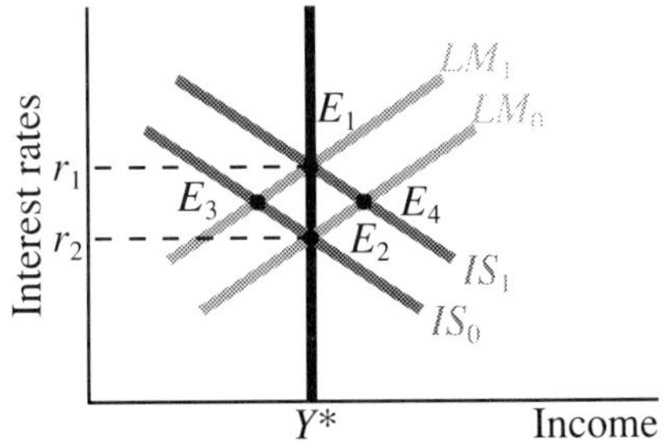

Slide 102 The composition of aggregate demand *(Figure 25-10)*

NOTES

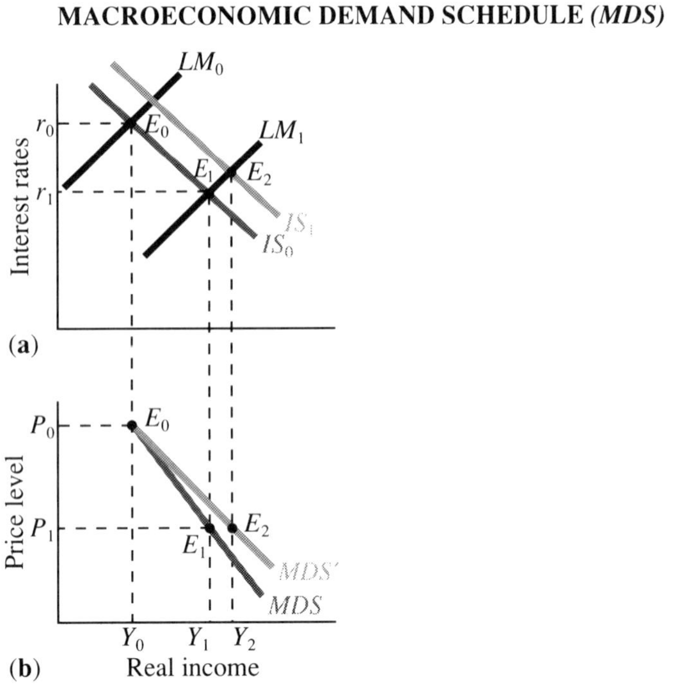

MACROECONOMIC DEMAND SCHEDULE (MDS)

(a)

(b)

Slide 103   Relaxing the fixed price assumption: the *MDS* (*Figure 26-1*)

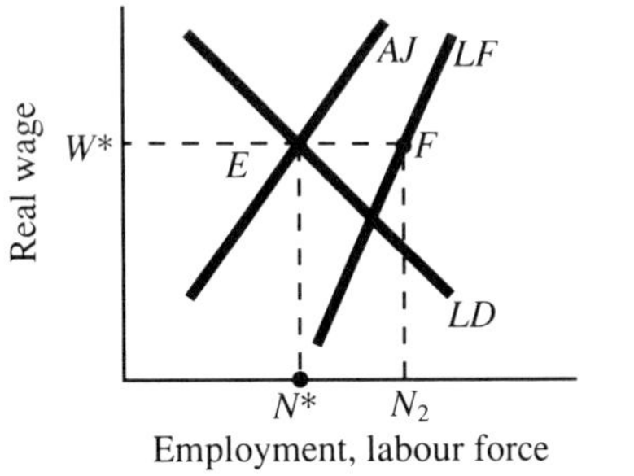

Slide 104   The labour market (*Figure 26-2*)

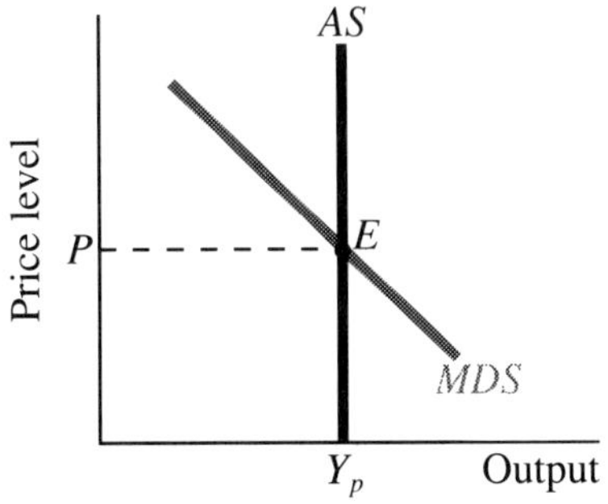

Slide 105   Aggregate supply and equilibrium (*Figure 26-3*)

55

NOTES

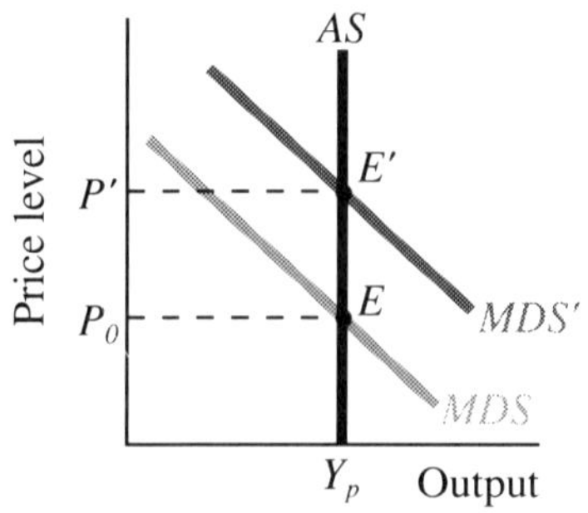

Slide 106   Monetary and fiscal policy *(Figure 26-4)*

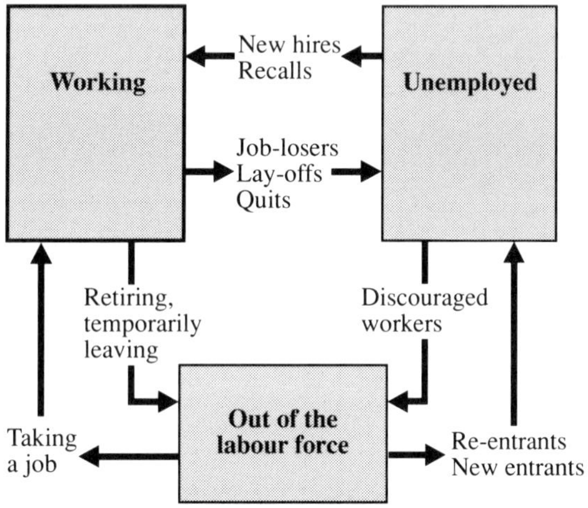

Slide 108   Labour market flows *(Figure 27-2)*

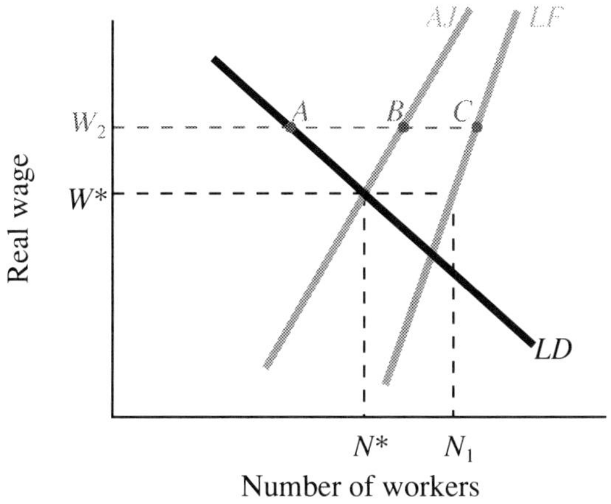

Slide 110   The natural rate of unemployment

57

NOTES

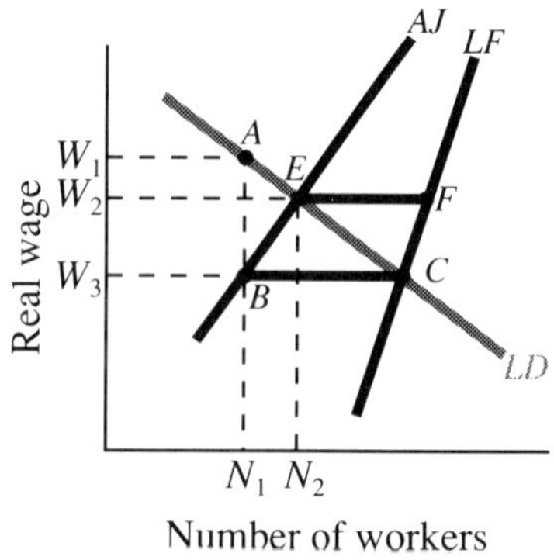

Slide 111   Will tax cuts reduce unemployment? *(Figure 27-4)*

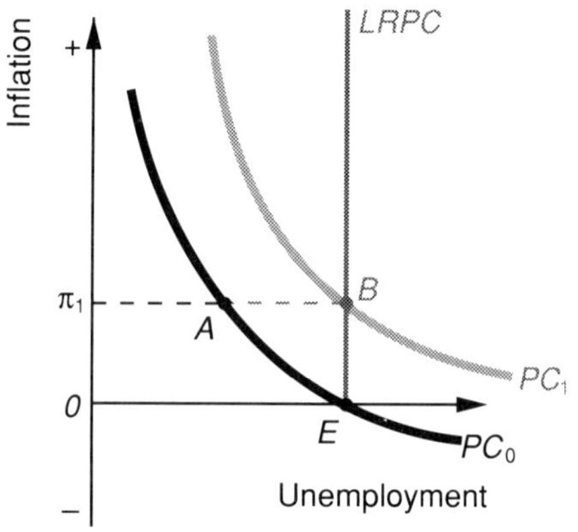

Slide 117   Inflation, unemployment and output

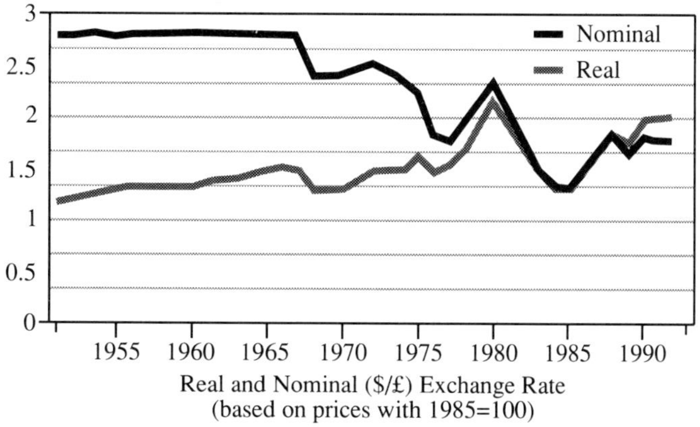

Real and Nominal ($/£) Exchange Rate
(based on prices with 1985=100)

Slide 122   International competitiveness

59

NOTES

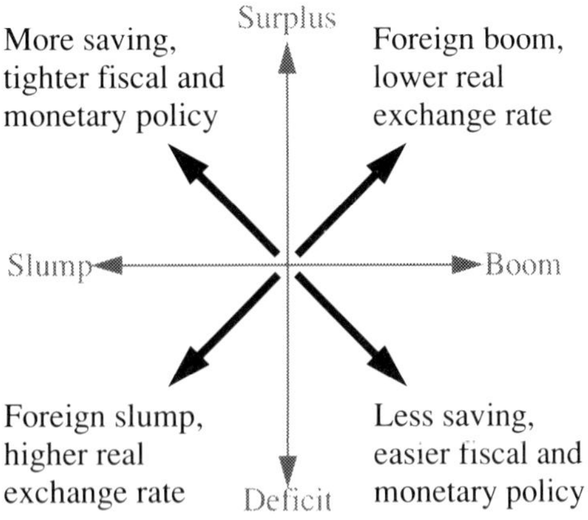

Surplus

More saving,
tighter fiscal and
monetary policy

Foreign boom,
lower real
exchange rate

Slump

Boom

Foreign slump,
higher real
exchange rate

Deficit

Less saving,
easier fiscal and
monetary policy

Slide 123   Internal and external balance *(Figure 29-3)*

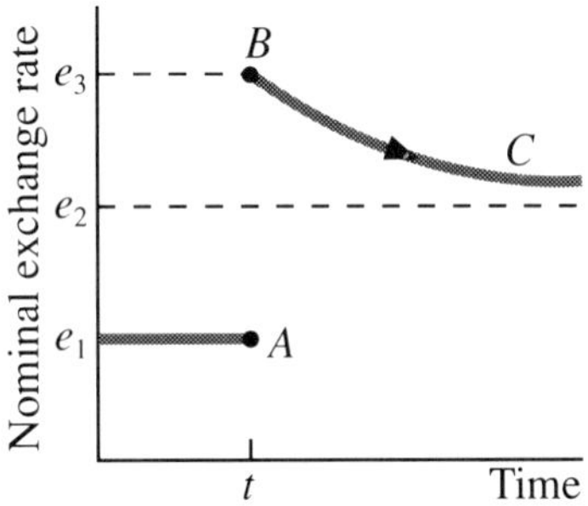

Slide 125   Policy options under *floating* exchange rates *(Figure 29-4)*

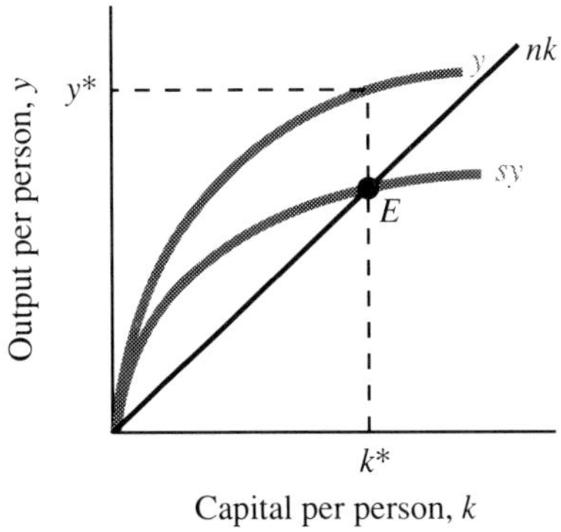

Slide 127   Theories of growth *(Figure 30-1)*

61

NOTES

C D

E

Trend output

B

A

Time

A—Slump
B—Recovery phase has begun
C—Boom
D—Recession under way
E—Slump again

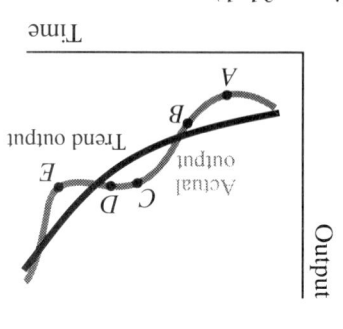

Slide 129   The business cycle *(Figure 31-1)*

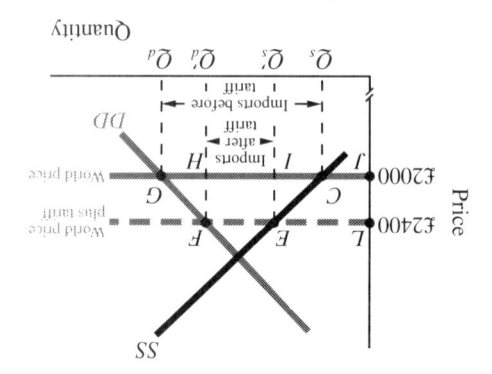

SS

Price

£2400 L   E   F   World price plus tariff
         C
£2000   Imports   World price
       J   I after   H
              tariff
         Imports before
              tariff
                              DD

Q_s Q'_s Q'_d Q_d

Quantity

Slide 134   Costs and benefits of a tariff *(Figure 33-3)*

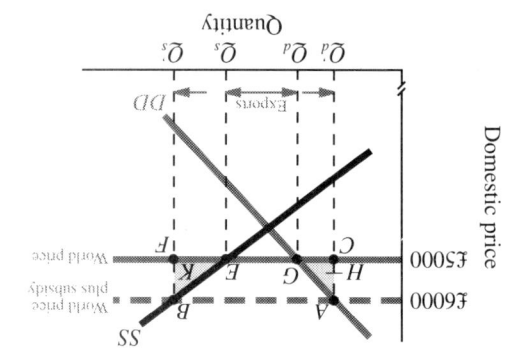

SS

£6000   A   B   World price plus subsidy
       H   G   E   K
£5000 C   F   World price

Domestic price

                  Exports
                              DD

Q'_d Q_d Q_s Q'_s

Quantity

Slide 135   Other commercial policy *(Figure 33-5)*

NOTES

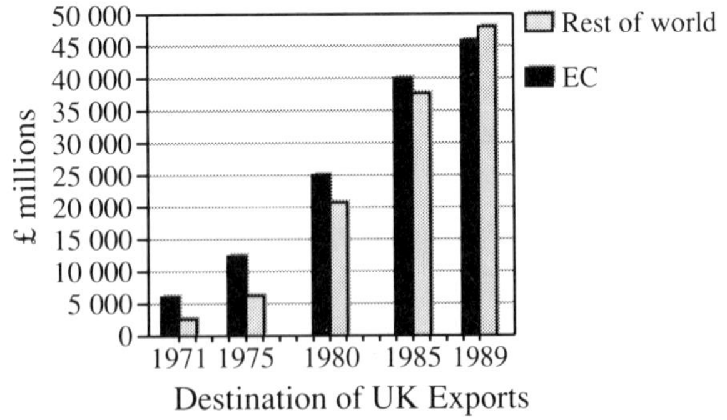

Slide 138 **European Monetary Union (EMU)** *(Source: AAS, Economic Review Data Supplement, Sept 1991)*

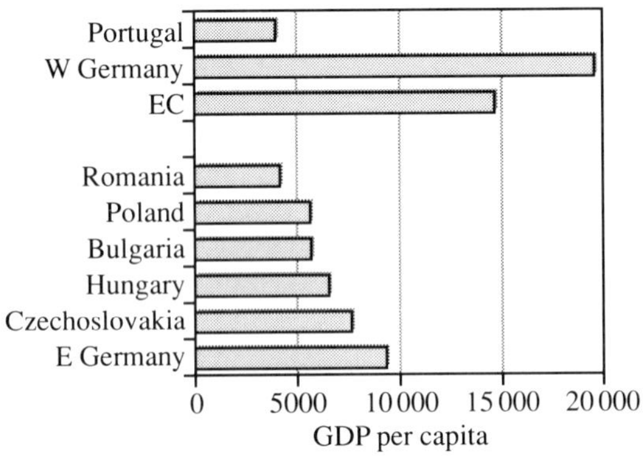

Slide 139 **Economic integration and Eastern Europe**

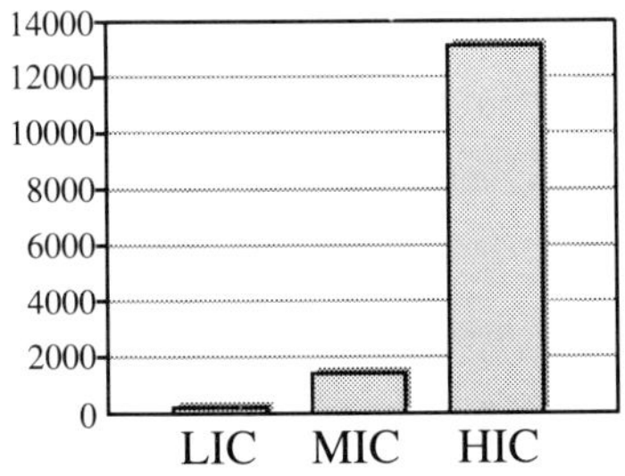

(a) GNP per capita 1990 (£)

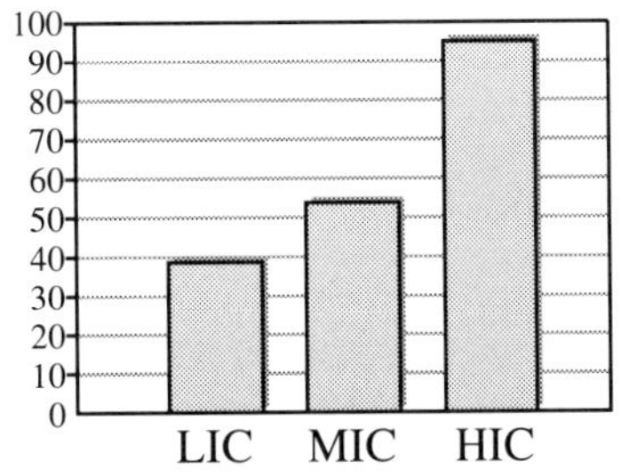

(b) % age group in sec education 1990

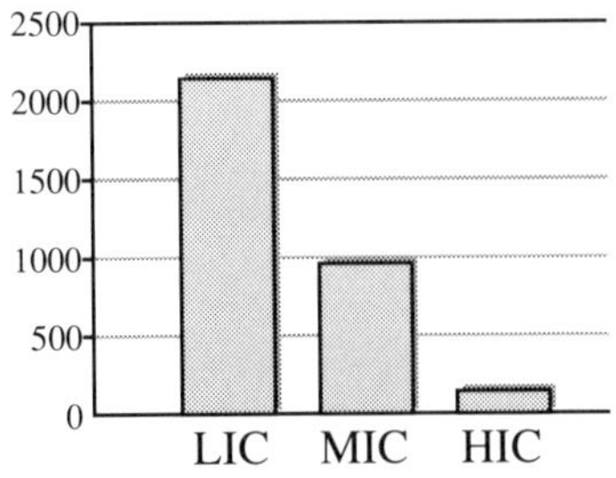

(c) Population per nurse 1984

Slide 140 **World income distribution**

65

NOTES

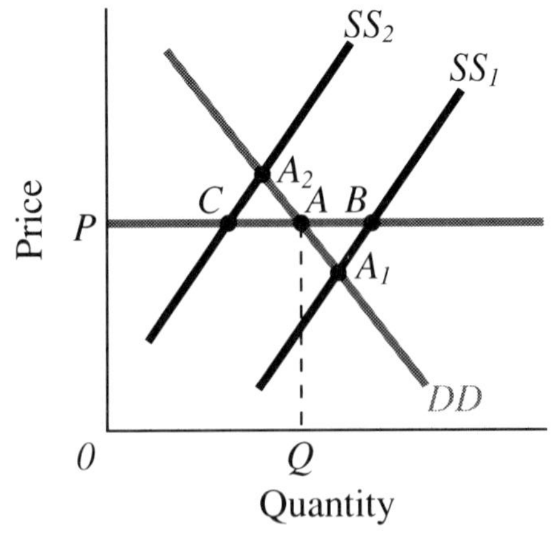

Slide 143   Commodity stabilization schemes *(Figure 36-1)*

NOTES

NOTES

NOTES

NOTES

NOTES

NOTES

NOTES